Lotus in the Stone

Sacred Journeys in Eternal India

Anuradha Goyal

गरुड

ISBN: 978-1-942426-34-9

Cover Design: Rakesh Chaudhary

Published by
Garuda Prakashan Private Limited
Gurugram, India
www.garudaprakashan.com
www.garudabooks.com

Printed in India

"No Indophile can afford to miss Anuradha Goyal's latest book *Lotus in the Stone – Sacred Journeys in Eternal India*. She interweaves a rich tapestry with threads drawn from our ancient spirituality, history and culture and colours it with a unique geographical context. At its very essence, this book re-affirms the enduring timelessness of India's living culture and speaks of India's cultural unity, transcending geographical distances as well as apparent differences."

Dr. Sumita Misra
Senior Advisor, Prime Minister's Economic Advisory Council, Author, Poet, Chair, Chandigarh Literary Society

"*Lotus in the Stone* is a marvellous book by Anuradha Goyal on the invisible threads that bind India's living civilization. Ostensibly a book on travels to sacred places, it goes beyond the recounting of the amusing experiences that constitute such journeys, to communicate the faith and connections to roots deep in the past. It shows India's sacred landscape as a veritable Indra's net, where each place reflects something of all the other places."

Prof. Subhash Kak
Author of The Circle of Memory and other books.

"This is a fascinating book. I have not read anything quite like this. Bharat, that is India, thrives in its people and its traditions. This is the legacy of samskriti or culture, carried beyond Indian shores to wherever Indians travelled. To appreciate and document this, a person has to travel beyond the dotted line, to where history and geography seamlessly weave together in this land of ours. I loved every word of the many lotuses in the many stones."

Bibek Debroy
Economist, author and translator of the Mahabharat

"This book is a pilgrimage through the consciousness of Indian civilization. The parikramas, the temple motifs, the sacred geographies, and ancient traditions are deftly woven by Anuradha into the story of a civilization built layer upon layer over thousands of years."

Sanjeev Sanyal
Economist, author of Land of the Seven Rivers

"A beautiful inspiring story and personal pilgrimage that teaches us how great Hindu temples unfold the secrets of the highest art and yogic spirituality relevant to each one of us. Anuradha Goyal's book Lotus in the Stone is a sacred journey through the inner time and space of these extraordinary temples to the Eternal and the Infinite."

Dr Frawley
Vedic scholar and author of numerous books

"An amazing book about Indian ancient traditions that resonate with our lives as if they recall events of yesterday. This is not just a book. It is a very reflective commentary on how ordinary people keep extraordinary traditions alive with respect, grace and a consideration for the Other. If one can respect diversity within in one's own cultural & religious traditions, one can also respect similar diversity of other faiths. A must-have for every student of inclusive, assimilative and living traditions."

Prof Anil Gupta
IIM Ahmedabad (retd), founder, Honey Bee Network

"India as a civilisation is united by its rich culture, pilgrimage centre, temples, our historical narratives, our great epics beneath the surface of a very diverse, multi-ethnic, multi-language, multi-custom society! Lotus in the Stone explains this beautifully, opening my eyes to our unity!"

T.V.Mohandas Pai
Aarin Capital Partners.

For

Shashi – The yantra, mantra and tantra of my life.

The greatest knowledge and the greatest riches man can possess are hers (India's) by inheritance; she has that for which all mankind is waiting.

– Sri Aurobindo

Contents

Stepping Out

योजनानां सहस्त्रं तु शनैर्गच्छेत् पिपीलिका।

—Subhashitamala

A distance of thousands of miles can be covered even by a tiny creature like an ant, if it keeps on walking slowly but consistently.

In the cold January winter, I was standing amidst a million strangers in Prayag, observing the transient world from a transient land as part of a cyclic event. The Kumbh Mela is a microcosm of the world, as it is created, lived, and dissipated. On the temporary flood plains created by the receding waters of the Ganga and the Yamuna, at the point of their confluence, a miniature world comes up for a couple of months. People from all over the country come here to spend time for various reasons. From curious tourists who want to see the Naga Sadhus to sadhus from different *akhadas* who come here to fulfil their periodic meeting with the world and with other sadhus, all kinds of people turn up at the Kumbh Mela. It is the longest living cultural tradition of India. The scale may have gone up or down during different phases of history, but it has continued unhindered. Its power lies in the fact that no one owns it, and at the same time, it belongs to everyone. It belongs to the one who turns up to be a part of it. No one invites anyone, and yet, everyone turns up on the banks of the holy rivers on the right date and time. In it, I also saw the power of the *panchang*, the Indian calendar in full force. Most of us who grow up in urban settings do not even know our birthdays by the panchang, but here, you see half of humanity turning up based on that very panchang. Is it the panchang's way of saying it still rules this land?

At the Kumbh Mela, I saw human behavior at its best ever. I was traveling alone and on the first day, I held my bag close to my chest. If someone decided to snatch it, it may be easier to find a needle in a haystack than a thief at the Kumbh Mela. Getting lost in the Kumbh Mela was a phrase embedded in our psyche by our filmmakers. Towards the end of the day, I loosened up and held my bag as freely as I would hold it anywhere else. By the next day, I could comfortably leave it on the side while having my chai at a tea stall. I knew no one was going to pick up my bag. This transformation in my own behavior in less than twenty-four hours was nothing less than magic. Hundred thousand so-called strangers around you, and you feel you are amongst your own family—this seems unbelievable, incomprehensible, until you feel it. I do not recall anyone touching me even by mistake during those few days that I was walking around the mela grounds, despite all the crowd. Policemen responded to queries with folded hands. There was free food for everyone, everywhere. Even at food stalls and chai shops, no one asked for money. When I tried to pay before I ate, they requested me to first eat and then pay, and only if I liked the food.

On an early morning boat ride to the *sangam*, there were just two women on the boat—me, and Kiran from Bihar who was there with her husband. They created a natural shield for me without any need of it, and without my asking for it. That day, I was just trying to capture some images of the sangam and had not really planned to take a dip in it. Kiran would listen to none of it and insisted that I must take a dip now that I had come to the sangam. When I told her that I was not carrying clothes to change into, she pulled out a sari from her bag and handed it over to me. I was hesitant, for we had met just then on the boat, and would probably never meet again after we got down from the boat. But she insisted, and I did take a dip in her sari, and she simply took back the wet sari and said she would dry it along with the rest of their clothes. This is not a social behavior we see very often, and I would totally understand if you do not believe me here; I too would have found this difficult to believe, if I had not experienced it myself.

I have worked in the space of business innovation earlier and have been a strong advocate of intersectional innovation which essentially says that creativity happens at the intersection of two different dimensions or spaces. The Kumbh Mela is a place where I literally saw this in action. Sadhus who have renounced the world come over here to meet the world. Most of them are inaccessible to people at large most of the time, but at the Kumbh Mela, you can just walk up to them and interact with them. Meanwhile, worldly people like me leave their worlds behind to lead the life of a sadhu here, for a while, as *kalpavasis*. These two sections of society meet at a place created temporarily by nature and by man, and it goes through a cycle every twelve years.

At the Kumbh Mela, artists of all kinds presented their poems, songs, and art works of all kinds, be it in the streets or inside the well-equipped tented auditoriums. Books and libraries were never far away. This was the world's largest conference happening in autopilot mode. Imagine how many ideas can take birth here.

This was utopia right in front of my eyes. I could trust anyone within the mela grounds even though I knew that the same person could behave differently just outside the grounds. Remember, no one was forcing us to behave, we behaved well on our own, driven by some deep-rooted inherent belief that most of us may not even be aware of. I cannot put my finger on the one thing that was creating this unbelievable environment. One just wishes that the mela grounds expanded to cover the entire world, and that its timeline expanded to match our lifetimes. Wishful, I know, but this is a place that gave me a lot of hope for the future. I had an absolute sense of belonging. It felt as if I was a part of each of the persons present there, and they of mine—a feeling I had never before experienced, and never later.

I guess this is a good juncture to look back at the incredible journey I have had, from being unaware of spiritual traditions to becoming someone who wants to spend the rest of her life exploring her own cultural roots—traveling across the sacred geography of India and reading the age-old wisdom in our scriptures.

India revealed herself slowly and steadily as I traveled across her mountains, rivers, coastlines, deserts, and ancient temple towns, and walked across her cosmopolitan cities. Every now and then, I discover aspects I was completely oblivious to. Every new visit to a place reveals a new dimension, no matter how small or insignificant the place may seem. The more I travel, the more I keep falling in love with this country that never ceases to amaze me. And this is what I share in this book. The India that I discovered, that has the sacred and eternal running all over her. The India I discovered, traveling across her, observing her marvels of art and architecture and thought, talking to the people who connect with her intimately, feeling an inexplicable thrill every time I grasped her myriad traditions and understood the multifold nuances of her temples and culture, all of it magically falling into place—the way seemingly chaotic patterns in a kaleidoscope do—into the sacred space-time the Kumbh brings forth.

Osho, in his book 'India My Love', says: "India is a paradox, constant images of contradictions. Hardly anything makes sense if one goes by logic, yet at another level, all seems to fall into place." I agree.

I have lived the most part of my life in India, in its different diverse parts, traveling to the nooks and corners of this country—for different reasons ranging from my father's regular transfers to business trips to personal pilgrimages—literally peeling the layers with every journey, discovering new stories. Connecting the dots of these stories brought out yet another layer of hidden stories that peeped out, teasing me for missing them earlier. Where does one begin talking about this enigma, this magic, this chaos, this mystery called India? The more you try to figure her out, the more she keeps showing you how much you do not know. So, let me begin by talking a bit about my own journey of discovering India.

Ironically, while growing up, I hardly knew India beyond the few cities that I grew up in. Those were the pre-internet, pre-mobile phone, even pre-telephone days; TV meant only Doordarshan, to which, in those days, most children had highly rationed access. Thankfully, due to the transferable job that my father had, I did get to live in multiple small towns across India. Glimpses of the rest of India came through textbooks, occasionally. Most of the general books I read then were either rooted in the past, like Amar Chitra Katha, or were pure fiction, like comics. Everything that I read in my textbooks did slot itself into my dream list of places to visit. I remember reading about the Ajanta Caves in my history textbook. When my father got posted to Aurangabad, it was the first visual that popped up in my mind.

My dadi went on an all-India train tour in her 60s. When she came back, she told me stories of temples big and distant. I knew I had to visit them, but I did not remember any other name except Rameshwaram because it kept featuring in the Ramayana story. She spoke about how people dressed differently, spoke differently, and ate things we had never heard of, but still prayed to the same deities. Without understanding any of those details, a quest to see them made home in my heart and mind. The traveler in her ignited the traveler in me.

I am a Hindu by birth, like billion plus other people on earth. Like most people of my generation—of the '70s and '80s—I was oblivious to this fact during my childhood. Add to this a childhood spent in army cantonments, and studying in Kendriya Vidyalaya where diversity is the norm, rather than an exception. My parents, during my growing-up years, were naturally plural, and respectful towards every kind of religious place and holy men and women. We were asked to pray for happiness whenever we were in the vicinity of God—be it a temple, gurudwara, church, or dargah, for God is everywhere and we must bow our head to every form divinity is worshipped in. This is how most people of that generation were, at least in North India where I grew up, and most of my friends did more or less what we did.

Having said that, I grew up primarily with my grandmother, who was a practicing Jain, but also read the Bhagavad Gita every day. Every morning and evening, she would wear her *muhnpatti*—a white piece of cotton cloth tied with a thread across her ears—to cover her mouth as she sat down to do her japa. Dadi in a white sari, white muhnpatti and white hair as she said her Namokara Mantra with a mala in her hands is what I remember of her. She would finish her daily japa by reading a chapter of the Bhagavad Gita. I still remember the red colored book in landscape format, with abridged chapters in very large font. Once every eighteen days, she would start from the first chapter. As I learnt to read, I started reading with her. I do not recall understanding anything, but even as a kid, I knew that it was something that gave her strength, and hence would give me strength too.

Growing up as a dark-skinned girl in fairness-obsessed Punjab, I came back crying from school one day, as someone called me "*Kali*". Dadi smiled and pointed out to me an image of Krishna standing next to his cow and playing his *bansuri*, which was on a wall of our home. She said, he was also "*Kala*", and we all worship him; so was Ram, so was Draupadi of Mahabharata fame, and so was Heer of Heer Ranjha love story fame. She told me, "*Gora* and Kala are two colors made by the same God, why should you be ashamed of having the same skin as the deities whom we worship?" That had me sorted for life on this issue. Subconsciously, this also built a bond between me and Krishna, who I thought was like me, so we could be friends and the thought stayed pretty much in my being for a long time. I do not remember any rituals, except maybe fasting on Janmashtami and Navaratri, which I mostly did for the sake of the rich food served after these fasts, which I really loved.

Visiting temples was sporadic for us and happened more when we travelled, though we did have a tradition of visiting a Hanuman temple on Tuesdays, when possible. There was a small temple at home, where we would do some pooja on Deepawali. Festivals were more of social events that included visiting people to wish and exchange sweets. I knew Gayatri Mantra and Hanuman Chalisa by heart, from a very young age, but I do not recall reciting any of them regularly.

I do not remember visiting many churches as a child, for there were not many of them around, but dargahs were more common. We would go there and bow, just as we did in temples. I had no idea that they were any different from temples, except that you got no prasad there. We used to visit gurudwaras regularly and memory of the *kada prasad* instantly pops up in my mind as I write this. The vast campus of the Golden Temple that I got to visit, its *sarovar* and its mild music stayed with me.

I am reminiscing spiritual nuggets from my growing-up days, so it may look like I led a deeply religious and spiritual life. Far from it, it was just a normal childhood of a middle-class Indian kid, focused on doing well at studies, for that was the only passport to getting a job for an economically stable future. In the mid '90s, I started working in India's nascent software industry. Life was good with enviable salaries, air-conditioned offices, and global opportunities.

A couple of years into the software industry, I joined the world's biggest FMCG company. Life moved from being comfortable to being luxurious. However, what thrilled me the most was that my job allowed me to travel across India, as the company had operations in more than forty-five locations across India.

My first ever two-week stay in Chennai is still fresh in my memory. I was awestruck when I saw the stone-carved temples of Mahabalipuram on a weekend. Women in my Chennai office used to wear fresh flowers in their hair, and this was a novelty for me. Marina beach became my 'go to' place, every evening and morning. I had never seen the sea before, and I wanted to feel it and take it in as much as possible. Little did I know that a few years down the line, I would be living next to the sea.

During my six-month internship in Pune, I lived in a girl's hostel in the narrow lanes of Narayan Peth, with five other girls, none of whom could speak anything other than Marathi, and I could not speak a word of Marathi. However, I cherish those six months of my life. By the time my internship ended, I started understanding Marathi to a large extent.

Pune was my first window not just to Maharashtra and Marathi culture, but also to the world south of the Vindhyas. I discovered that *gol gappe* was not just called pani puri, but also served with hot masala instead of the ice-cold water that I was used to. I saw Birju Maharaj performing with

Ustad Zakir Hussain on the tabla one evening; other evenings were spent attending music concerts, plays, etc. All this was so new and so enriching for me. Now, I hardly remember the software skills I picked up then, but the culture I soaked in has become a part of me.

On the weekends, I would go trekking up the Maratha hill forts. However, I missed visiting Shaniwar Wada despite having lived very close to it and passing by it almost every day. I am not even sure if it was open to the public then. I had no clue of its historical importance and no one in Pune spoke to me about it. When talking about Puneri things, all we knew was Chitale Bakarwadi—the popular sweet and salt snack from the city.

While the Pune stint was an experience that I just lived through, my travels during my IT career started giving me glimpses of the vast diversity of India. No matter how much you read about India in books, or binge watch on television or on the web, nothing comes close to the experience that you get with your own five senses. When you breathe in the air that carries not just the smell, but also the essence of a culture, when you see the colors with your own eyes, feel the taste of the food on your tongue and jump at the spice or sugar levels, you become a part of the place and it becomes a part of you for the rest of your life. I started looking forward to my travels.

In 2002, I moved to Bangalore and Bangalore became the fertile ground that nurtured my wanderlust. It allowed me to travel a bit, including a few stints outside India. Out-of-India stints did two things for me. First, they allowed me to look at India from outside. I remember a client manager in UK asking me about how our office was in India. He was curious and a bit condescending, for India's public image remained that of a poor country. I logged on to my company's website and showed him our office; all he could say was, "You are embarrassing me. We are making you work in an awful box-like office." When I told him that every morning, I had my breakfast sitting next to a luxury swimming pool, I saw his opinion of India change instantly and saw the emergence of respect for our team and for India in his eyes. In the same office, a lady director, who was roughly my mother's age, had a daughter my age, who was getting married. She had constant anxiety about the wedding arrangements. When she spoke about the upcoming wedding, I saw that she could be any mother in India. She was worried about the expenses, the wedding gown that must fit perfectly, about the guest list. I suddenly realized that some common threads exist across the world. This was just the beginning of my discovery that, at a human level, our emotions are always the same, no matter how different we may be externally. Later, during my couchsurfing days, I met women from across the world and I realized that their challenges and anxieties in life were just the same as mine as a single working woman.

Couchsurfing brought the world to my doorstep. Sometime in 2006 I got introduced to the then newly launched concept that let you stay with locals, with no commerce of any kind involved. You could also host travelers visiting your city. This sounded surreal to begin with, but as I started hosting people, I started enjoying it. Every other day, I had guests from some corner of the world living in my guest room. In those early days, it was used by true blue travelers only, though freeloaders would soon follow. If I was enjoying my travels at every possible opportunity, I was as much enjoying the world traveling to my house, chatting with me over cups of chai, telling me stories of their worlds while we cooked meals together.

In 2004, I discovered blogging. I was traveling and reading books in my free time, and my reactions to both went into my blog. Blog became my new playground that let my words reach an unknown audience across the globe. People started reacting to my posts, some even started asking me to write on specific topics and visit certain places. This was thrilling. People were not just reading me, they were responding to me, and they were adding to my knowledge.

Somewhere along the way, photography joined the game. As mobile technology evolved, videos happened, social media channels popped up, but my blog firmly stayed as the locus of my digital existence.

For a few years, I was traveling mostly in South India over weekends and vacations—sometimes with friends, and sometimes alone. With every trip, every blog, and through responses to it, I discovered something new. It was as if a conspiracy was pushing me in a direction that I had no inkling of. This was when I explored much of India. I did long solo trips to places like Bhutan and Sikkim when they were yet to open to tourism. The only aspect that remains constant in each of my trips is that I discover there is so much more in a place to see, explore, observe, and experience. I visit a place with a mental list of things to see in a place, but I always come back with a longer list that demands another visit, longer than this one.

As I moved out of formal employment, and soon after that from Bangalore to Gurgaon, I had more time to travel and write. Come the second decade of the 21st century, the tourism industry woke up to bloggers. Tourism boards and hospitality brands started inviting bloggers on media trips. This was good, though eventually, I would discover the strings that come attached with it and the unease it brings along.

I did an introductory course in Indian Art at the National Museum Institute located at the National Museum in New Delhi. This course opened doors to the world of Indian Art for me. Just about forty hours spread over six months, but it had a great impact on me. The fact that we could see in the museum almost everything that the professors spoke about made it fascinating. I knew I could spend a lifetime exploring India.

My travels started getting focused. I realized it was heritage that fascinated me the most. Not that I did not enjoy nature and wildlife, but stones and ruins spoke to me. I felt they were telling me stories that I must tell the world. I almost felt responsible for telling their stories. My small stints outside India, coupled with my *bania* genes and business consulting background, made me see the opportunity for tourism products in each of them.

After the Indian art course, I became aware of art forms, be it sculptures, paintings, folk arts, decorative arts, textiles, or a combination of them. Now, wherever I went, I could not only see the layers of art in everything, but also understand it to a large extent. I could look at Ajanta paintings, understand its nuances and even explain it to people around me. I always liked museums, but now they held far more meaning for me, now I knew how to look at and appreciate an artefact from another time and space. My focus further narrowed down to ancient Indian art and civilization. This led me to explore ancient temples, and over time, I became more and more interested in them.

At another level, initially, my travels were for entertainment, a leisure activity. Soon, curiosity became the prime driver, and it kept getting more intense and eventually took the shape of an exploration. In my early days of exploration, it was unstructured and random, but slowly, my pre-trip readings and research started giving structure to my travels. Today, traveling is an exhausting exercise wherein I hardly sleep, charged up by discovering all that the destination decides to share with me.

Writing about my travels on my blog helped me in many ways, the biggest being my improved sense of observation. I often hear my co-travelers say that they were on the same trip, but they never noticed all that I wrote in the blog. While it was a kind of documentation for me, it helped me connect with people who would then give me more information on the places I should explore. This became a spiral of discovery, exploration, observation, experience, and blogging.

During my growing-up days in North India, nice and beautiful temples meant the ones made in white marble, with *murtis* in white marble and a matching floor to walk on. The whiter the temples, the purer they felt. I think the first stone monument I saw were the Ellora Caves in the early '90s, when my father was posted in Aurangabad. However, my mind read them more as ruins, rather than temples. Then came the temples of South India—in bare hard stone with rigid priests who would not think twice before shouting you down if need be. My first reaction to stone temples was cold. They did not fit into my worldview of beautiful temples. The stone was too hard compared to the delicate marble. The *garbhagriha* too dark, too far away, with multiple doorways between me and the deity. Priests were too rude and too rigid. I do not recall registering any of the carvings or stories that I would later rave about. I did register that people visiting temples in South India took it far more seriously than people in the North. I never saw any frivolous behavior in South Indian temples. Women wore their best silks to temples here, even better than the ones they wore to weddings.

I started discovering different aspects of temple architecture, different architectural styles and stories sculpted in stone all over. I fell totally in love with temples. I could find beauty in the smallest and most simple looking temples. Every time I looked at an ancient temple, I thought of the one who commissioned it, the one who designed it, the one who planned it, the one who chiseled it, and the generations who prayed in it. How much devotion and commitment you would need to build even a small temple! Over time, I learnt the nuances of temples across India and some outside India too.

Then came the temple stories—why were these temples built where they are? Is there a sacred geography they are a part of? What are the different types of temples? Ask an expert and he would most probably categorize temples based on their architectural styles, or perhaps based on the presiding deity of the temple or the stone used to build it or the period it was built in. For a while, I too chased these categories in the temples I visited. I would soon realize that all of these are just data points about a temple and a temple is not these data points. These are just measures, for those who see the temple as just a physical entity. Temples are that too, but that is not their essence.

On these temple trails, I had my moments of spiritual rendezvous. I was in Khajuraho with my family once. Destinations anyway keep me awake during my travels, so I walked up to the western group of temples early morning at sunrise. We had seen them come alive the previous night at the light-and-sound show, but I was yet to see them in daylight. I walked into the premises, walking past the plaque declaring it as a world heritage site, and the lovely sculpted temples all around fought for my attention. Lost in the poetry-in-stone scattered all around, I walked around to feel the place. I stopped in front of the Kandariya Mahadev Temple, just as the first rays of the sun were falling on it. It shimmered as if it was made of delicate sandalwood and not stone. Not too big in size, it looked like a toy playing with the sunrays. Everything else merged into the background—it was just the temple and the sunrays in front of my eyes. Some resonance, or *spandan* as they say in Sanskrit, happened, and I had tears in my eyes. I felt the rhythm of the architecture of the *shikhara*—many small peaks leading to the big peak, a re-creation of the Kailash Parvat, the home of Shiva—inside me. I stood still and tears kept flowing from my eyes. I have no explanation for what happened, I only know that something happened and my relationship with temples had changed forever.

A similar experience repeated a few years later. I was on a Chola temple trail, visiting Mahabalipuram,

Chidambaram, Kumbakonam, and then at the pinnacle of our trip—Thanjavur. Here too, we reached in the evening and visited the Brihadeeswara Temple early in the morning, just as sunrays were painting it red. The temple is huge, beautiful, overpowering, overwhelming and mesmerizing—all at once. We walked around carrying the ASI guidebook in hand, looking at sculptures and thanking Rajaraja Chola for creating such a masterpiece. A bit tired, I sat at the Nandi Mandapa, telling my friend, "Let's see how Nandi looks at Shiva from here." As soon as I looked at the temple from the Nandi Mandapa, I felt the rhythm in the stone in front of me resonate with my inner rhythm, and again, I had tears flowing from my eyes for no reason. I tried to hold back my tears, but my tears stopped only when I got up from that spot and moved to another spot. There is no way I can explain this, and now, I do not even see a need to explain what I experienced at these two, thousand plus-year-old temples separated by a distance of two thousand kilometers. What I do know is that some rehashing took place inside me.

A major transformation happened inside me when I visited Ayodhya for the first time. It was a media trip organized by Uttar Pradesh Tourism with a choice of different itineraries. In the fairly large group, it was just me and two European journalists who chose to visit Ayodhya. I was driven by intrigue. Ayodhya as a city had dominated news headlines since my childhood, but none of them spoke about the city beyond the conflict for the Ram Janambhumi site. I wanted to see the city where one of our two epics took place. The European journalists were driven by the storyline they had been commissioned to write for a magazine. After spending more than half a day in Faizabad looking at some medieval monuments, we finally reached the Guptar Ghat from where we took a boat to Ayodhya.

The skyline of Ayodhya slowly made an appearance as if emerging out of the Sarayu River. I vividly remember landing at the Jhumki Ghat and finding neat clean ghats lining the banks of the Sarayu. We were greeted with flower garlands and taken to two temples—Hanuman Garhi and Kanak Bhawan. At Kanak Bhawan, I read a board that lists the renovations of the temple since the time it was built. It mentions every date and every person associated with the renovation, right up to the last one by the queen of Orchha. Was the temple telling me the history of Ayodhya through its own history? We walked through the colorful lanes of Ayodhya before sitting for a meal in an ashram.

While having the meal, I asked my guide about the Ram Janambhumi Temple and if it was accessible? He politely told me that it was not on the itinerary. I knew it even before I chose to visit Ayodhya that the Ram Janambhumi Temple was not on the itinerary. However, once I stepped into Ayodhya, I had this strong urge to visit it. Was it the impact of being in the vicinity of the temple? I do not know. All I know is, by the time I finished my meal, I felt I had to visit the temple. There was a reluctance in everyone to take me there. So, I told them that I would visit the temple on my own and make my own arrangements to return to Lucknow. It is just 130 kilometers away, after all. Travelling 130 kilometers is not a big deal.

They finally gave in and took me to the temple. I went through multiple security checks that bordered on violation, even when I had left everything behind and had taken just my wallet with me. I walked through the narrow lanes fenced by iron barricades. Monkeys were jumping atop the barricades. At some point in the queue, I saw people turning to their right, folding their hands in prayer before being told to move ahead. When my turn came, I went numb. My hand went up in prayer like everyone else, and tears started flowing out of my eyes. I fought to control my tears, but my eyes would not listen, it was like Ganga-Jamuna flowing from my eyes. The priest looked at me sympathetically; he was probably used to this reaction. I saw a dusty tent on top of rubble at a distance of 30–40 meters. The priest was sitting closer to the queue and would give a bit of prasad to everyone. Surely, a deity revered across India, whose name is taken to greet one another, and whose name is taken at the last journey cannot be treated like this, I felt. As I looked across that fence, I did not know if he was in jail, if I was in jail, or if both of us were in our respective jails. At that moment, I realized I am a Hindu. It moved me so deeply that I was restless for a long time. Stepping out of the temple, walking to the car, I knew I had to come back to spend some time in Ayodhya. By the time I returned from the trip, it was a resolve to study Ayodhya in detail.

It took me two years to go back to Ayodhya, but this time I had all the time to explore it. I read the Ayodhya Mahatmay of Skand Puran that gave me a long list of temples, ponds, and ashrams in Ayodhya. I went searching for them—for temples, and for the living culture of this oldest city in India. This time, I visited Ram Janambhumi on the penultimate day of my trip when I was quite soaked in Ayodhya. I was prepared to see what I saw the previous time. This time, it was a trip to the presiding deity of the land, like paying respect to the eldest person of the family you are visiting. I went through the security rigmarole—calm, composed and a bit jovial, if I may say so. I stood before the tent housing Sri Ram Lalla in bright purple clothes and told the priest, "Now, I have seen him twice in the tent, tell him, next time I want to see him in a temple." He smiled, indulging me as elders do with kids asking for big things beyond them. The commando standing inside holding a large gun in his hands, wearing a black bandana and a black uniform turned around with his gun and said, "Madam, *Mandir to yahin banega*—the temple will be built right here." I smiled and said, "You are the Hanuman of this age and if you say so, so will it be." He turned to do his duty, guarding Ram Lalla just like how Hanuman would have done in another age.

About a year later, the day the Ayodhya verdict came, it was this commando's face and words that kept ringing in my head. I could imagine his pain of standing there, guarding the Ram Janambhumi, with an urge to build it, but bound by protocol to just stand there and watch. I feel it is the *seva* of people like him that has been answered. *Mandir wahin banayega* and *Mandir wahin banega* has dominated both mainstream and social media as slogans, but for someone to stand there and believe in it so passionately connected me even more to the intensity of the moment.

Lately, I have been visiting temples as a devotee, as a seeker, as someone who absorbs the energy created by thousands of devotees before me and someone who adds her energy to the temples visited. The stories associated with the temples have become important to me. Most old temples were built with a purpose and you rarely see a randomly built temple. I started discovering the sacred geography of ancient temple towns of India. There are too many of them to visit in a lifetime. I read the Dwarka Mahatmay before visiting Dwarka and the Mathura Mahatmay before visiting Mathura. Even though I have visited Kashi—as Varanasi was called since ancient times—multiple times, I know I am yet to explore it as per the Kashi Khand of Skand Puran. The same goes for Bhubaneshwar, Ujjain, Nashik, and many other temple towns. These are not just temples but spaces that are deeply inherent to our culture, literature and fabric, something I was totally ignorant of, all these years.

My travels were like scratching a scratch card with nails; scratching away the label you need to remove to see what luck has in store for you. Before you see the entire surface, you have to scratch open many windows. The more windows you open, the more the surface intrigues you. I was opening such windows with my travels. Every time, a little more of the surface was revealed. I wondered what India would have looked like before the invasions started changing the landscape here. I was specially intrigued by the 10–11th century landscape when the most exquisite architecture was built across the length and breadth of the country. To me, this comes across as the golden period of India, something that probably attracted the evil eye. Did the people of then forget to do the rituals to protect all this from the evil eye?

This yearning to know how India would have been kept growing. I could not see a window that gave me the hope of seeing good old India where everyone behaved themselves, acted as per their dharma and lived in perfect harmony. It was a wish that I had almost no hope of being fulfilled.

I was holding a lot of threads in my hands, but they were just not coming together to form a fabric. Each thread had a story, or a subplot, but until they were woven together, the whole picture would not be visible. A picture, as we know, is more than the sum of its parts.

The answer came when I visited the Kumbh Mela at Prayagraj. The few days that I spent on the banks of the Ganga-Yamuna in the cold January let me glimpse the whole picture. That was when all the threads that I had been collecting along my decades of travel came together to form the fabric that is India. It was then that everything fell into place and I began to understand India and saw beneath her complexity. All those temples I visited, the sacred geography I tread, the pilgrimages I ventured, the art and architecture I relished, the traditions and festivals that I marveled across the length and breadth of this sacred land were leading up to this moment. I knew this is the hologram of the larger picture that would emerge when we have scratched away all the layers of this magical scratch card. Will this image appear in my lifetime? I do not know, but I wish it does. Will it happen? Yes, it will.

It has been an exciting and enlightening journey. Come, join me, as I retrace my footprints across this mystical land.

Beneath the Veneer

आस्ते भग आसीनस्य, ऊध्वस्तिर्ष्ठति तिष्ठतः।
शेते निपद्यमानस्य, चराति चरतो भगः।।

—Aitareya Brahman 7.15

The fate of a person who sits, also sits. The fate of a person who stands, also stands. The fate of a sleeping person also sleeps. And the fate of a person who walks, also walks forward (expands).

Pictures of a leading film celebrity at a Durga Puja Pandal, praying to the Devi along with his family, were going viral on social media. The images generated a huge response, mostly of admiration, from his huge fan base across age groups. It was a picture-perfect family moment, and we in India love such images. In the middle of all this adulation, someone pointed out that the said gentleman had been making tall claims of not following any religion and of being "just an Indian" on various public platforms. Another comment pointed out how, many people like to present themselves as "atheists" or "spiritual but not religious," but engage in extensive rituals and regularly visit temples in their private lives. Does this remind you of anyone in your own circle of family and friends who does the same? Well, it reminded me of many such people I have come across. By the same token, I am sure you remember those crucial moments when exam results were expected, when we folded our hands and prayed to all possible deities, even if we did not pray for the rest of the year?

This is typical of Hindus in India. We keep our faith private and stay as neutral as possible, almost atheistic, in public. This may have come from the fact that we have multiple faiths co-existing. The paths within the Hindu faith are also divergent enough, and we hardly know about the ones we do not follow. I think this stems from the deep-rooted faith that the relationship between you and your *ishta devata* is personal and intimate. At a temple, when hundreds of people are standing in front of a murti, each one of them is praying directly to that deity, without any mediator between them. They are probably not even praying, but having a conversation with the deity, telling their problems, sharing their joys and sorrows, and asking for advice or guidance. This is not a congregation; it is a personal space even though it is public and shared with millions of people who visit the same temple to talk to the same deity. So, does our faith connect us together at some level, even while it lets us be our own individual selves?

During my travels, at times I managed to delve below this veneer and got glimpses of how, somewhere deep down, our faith does connect us to each other. Allow me to take you along some such journeys with me.

I had taken a pre-paid taxi from Varanasi airport. My hotel was an hour away, it was late at night, thanks to a much-delayed flight. I turned on my live location for my family to track me reaching the hotel. Once settled, the driver and I got into a conversation. For him, I was a potential customer for the duration of my stay in the pilgrim city. He started telling me about the usual touristy places that I could visit in Kashi. I told him I wanted to visit Vindhyachal and Meerjapur. These places are close to Bhadohi, a place famous for its hand-woven carpets. He asked me if I wanted to buy carpets. He was recalibrating me as a customer—probably not a tourist or a pilgrim, but a businesswoman or a handicraft enthusiast. When I said I wanted to visit Vindhyavasini Devi along with Ashtbhuja

Devi and Kali Khoh, his instant response was— "*Aap Mai ke dwar jayengi*?" meaning "Will you visit the home of the Mother?"

From then onwards, our conversation was all about Ma Vindhyavasini. He told me he visited her temple at least fourteen times a year—every purnima or full moon day, and during both the Navaratris. This apart, if any opportunity presented itself for his visiting the temple, he would grab it. He spoke with absolute devotion for the Devi. He told me how his father used to visit the temple like how he does now, and that after him, his son would continue the tradition. He had no doubts at all that his son would take over from him. In his devotion-soaked voice, he said, he had been driving for more than forty years by now and had never had an accident so far, not even a scratch on any of his cars, as he believed that the hands driving the car might be his, but the car was being driven by "*Mai*". She took care of him, his car, his family, and he just had to follow what she told him to do.

I wondered if he visited Kashi Vishwanath every day, since it is pretty much within the city of Varanasi, and for visitors, it is the most important temple in town. He was silent for a while, and after a pause, he said, "We do not have the courage to approach the father directly, we must reach him through the mother only." This is the simplest way to convey what a number of rishis, saints, sages, and philosophers have tried to tell us down the ages, I feel. Scholars have written piles of books to explain this simple relationship between Shiva and Shakti. A common Indian understands this, not just from the metaphor he sees at his home, where children usually reach the father via the mother, but also because he instinctively understands the way the cosmos works. The way to reach Shiva is through Shakti, his *maya*, his power of manifestation.

I next asked him how many pilgrims he had taken to the temple town of Vindhyachal so far. To my surprise, he said, "In my forty plus years of driving, you are the first person who wants to go to Vindhyachal." Mind you, it is just a ninety-minute drive from Varanasi, one of the most visited cities in India. He insisted that he would take me there and show me all the temples, but this time his voice conveyed to me that he was not seeing me as a mere customer, but as a fellow devotee who had not yet visited Mai and must be taken to her, and must receive the grace of Mai, just like him. I was a fellow Mai's child—a sibling. After this conversation, I felt so comfortable with him that I found it ridiculous that I had earlier shared my live location with my family while traveling with this man. This is how faith sometimes connects you and comforts you.

A few days later, when I was back in Goa, I and my husband were walking around in the hinterlands of Goa, chasing birds. We stopped at a small roadside tea stall wherein only two other men were there, having chai. I heard them conversing in a dialect of Eastern Uttar Pradesh and asked them where they were from. As expected, they said, "Uttar Pradesh." People of Uttar Pradesh believe, and maybe rightly so, that the rest of India looks at their state as a single unit. When I probed further, they told me they were from Ghazipur that is about one hundred and fifty kilometers from Vindhyachal. I told them that I had recently been to Vindhyachal, and both instantly said, "*Aap pahunch gayi Mai ke paas*" meaning "So, you have reached the Mother." I took out my phone and showed them the images of those temples. Their hands instantly folded in reverence, and an emotion of happiness filled their eyes. They kept repeating, "*Aap Mai ke paas pahunch gayi.*" Initially, I reckoned their comment as—So, you visited the Mother—the way we would voice it to someone bragging about their travels. But later, I realized, this is not what they meant. They meant that I had received a certain amount of divine blessing to have reached there—you cannot reach that place unless Mother wants you to come, and if she wants you to come, it is her blessing. Needless to say, we were both happy for that small tea-time conversation before heading our own ways.

On a media trip in Kerala, I had kept aside a day for exploring the city of Kochi, especially its ancient temples. There was a young journalist who had also stayed back for a day but had not really planned her day. She asked me if she could join me for the Kochi exploration. I told her that I was going to temples and would take my own sweet time to explore them, so if she were okay with that, she could come along. I must admit I was skeptical. With the stereotypical image I carried of young journalists, I had expected her to be more interested in current affairs, rather than ancient temples. But then, she said, yes, she would be interested. And sure enough, she was right there at the lobby at 6 a.m. to leave with me for our Kochi temple trail. As we went from temple to temple, looking at their unique architecture and unique practices like the Cracker Puja at the Chottanikkara Temple or the Vamanamoorthy Temple associated with the legend of Mahabali, I was worried if this would be too much for a young girl. She surprised me by the way she spent time over each temple, the way she said her prayers—with absolute devotion. I could see her happiness at discovering so many temples, including the one associated with the Onam legend, as Onam was around the corner. At the end of the day, she was grateful that she had discovered so many temples which she hadn't even known to have existed, and would have never been on her itinerary, had she planned it herself. She spoke with nostalgia about her grandfather who was a pujari, and how he used to do puja every day with fresh flowers, when she picked up flowers from the flower sellers outside each temple. She had a trip down memory lane; in a way, it served as a reminder to her to stay glued to her faith, perhaps a bit more actively. Well, she is one of those young Indians, still rooted in deep reverence for the deities they grew up with, but all of this beneath the veneer of being modern Indians who are spiritual but not religious.

A similar thing happened when two young bloggers from Lucknow joined me for a day trip to Naimisharanya. They joined me more because they wanted to travel with me, a little more established blogger than them, and it was just a day trip. I remember we were at the ancient Bhuteshwar Mahadev Mandir for the morning arti. The priest, for some reason, allowed us to stay inside the temple during the arti, while he pushed many people out. We spent 10–15 minutes at the arti, inside that small temple with a big Shivalinga that is surrounded by ancient murtis in black stone, of Mahavishnu, Durga, Ganesha and Surya. This intense ritual that engaged all our senses had a dramatic effect on all of us. The first words I heard from the young boys as we stepped out were, "That was amazing." They went on to recall how many times their parents had insisted on their attending the arti, which they had never bothered to. I saw that they had a tinge of regret for having missed out on this experience for so long. In their later blogs and writings, I saw a distinct respect emerging for temples and spiritual places. Such an instant connection could happen only if it had existed in one's system but had been lying recessive somewhere. Later, they would tell me that they had gone back to the same temple, just to attend the arti again.

Back home in Goa, I get two sets of visitors. One set, my in-laws, to be precise, primarily come to visit their Saraswat *kul devata* temples. They mostly come, stay at the temples, perform the pujas as planned, visit us for a meal or a cup of tea, and go back. Another set comprises my friends from my student days, corporate days, and my social media friends. They come to Goa to chill out and have a dream holiday. I am often asked to suggest the new things they could do in Goa, expectedly so, as I run a reasonably well-read travel blog. To this set, when I suggest visiting temples, they usually say, "Oh no, we are not the 'temple kind'" or "We are not into religion" or "We are spiritual but not religious." Sure, I tell them. When I help them with their itinerary, I find that they always have a small window of time which they camouflage as—We have to meet someone, or, we have some urgent work to take care of. Sooner or later, I figure out that they did pay a visit to the temples during this window of time. I now find it amusing that they keep their temple visits under wraps. The only logical answer I can think of is that they want to keep the rendezvous between them and their deity strictly personal and private. However, I just have to go back in time and imagine being in their shoes, to remember that visiting temples had never been cool, and certainly not when you are visiting a cool place like Goa. I am not here to say if people should or should not talk about their faith with others. We all choose to do what we do based on our life experiences. As an observer, what I see here is a faith that is still practiced, even if they wish to keep it away from the public eye. Are we afraid of being judged? Maybe!

Sometime back, on my twitter timeline, appeared a tweet by Dr. Subramanian Swamy wherein he shared an interesting fact—that Periyar EVR, who is known to be anti-religion, and anti-brahmin, had actually kept a vow he had made to his parents, that he would maintain their ancestral family temple in his hometown of Erode. He was talking about the 10th century Chola temple that Kasthuri Ranganatha Perumul dedicated to Vishnu, which incidentally has won awards for being the best maintained temple several times from the Government of Tamil Nadu. In response to this tweet, many people posted newspapers reports confirming the same, that whatever Periyar may have stood for in his public life, he never cut off his ties with his family deity whom he served as required by their family lineage. Eventually, Dr. Swamy said exactly what I wish to say here—people of Tamil Nadu visit temples more than anyone else, and this is where anti-Hindu rhetoric flourishes more than anywhere else! He said this about Tamil Nadu, but to a different extent, this can be seen across India. Deep down, we are connected to our deities and the lineage that we are born into, but we may choose to present an image that is entirely opposite of it. How we manage this dichotomy is a matter for exploration, but not in this book!

Through other episodes, I discovered that our common faith has the ability to connect us together deeply. Connections to traditions are actually as strong as they seem to be fragile. There have been times when I sensed this connection with people who are strangers or near strangers, while traveling, just because we had discovered our underlying common faith. Sometimes, there was a professional relationship between me and the other person, but the common faith made us trust each other more easily, we felt we could depend on each other far more easily. I do not have a formal guru or follow any of the popular gurus in India today. However, these observations made me understand what connects the followers of various spiritual gurus—a family-like bonding, where the glue is the common belief in the guru or lineage you follow together.

On a trip to explore the city of Haridwar, I was being hosted by the Uttarakhand Tourism Development Board. An exceptionally talented lady from the board was accompanying me. She is one of the most enterprising persons I have ever met in the public sector—sharp, focused, passionate, and working hard for her organization. We kept discussing about increasing the flow of tourists to Uttarakhand, and our conversations were more oriented towards business. I had gone there to study the city of Haridwar as one of the ancient cities of India, so I was visiting a number of ancient temples around the city. She, being busy with her work, would stay in the car doing her work while I visited temples and spoke to priests and pilgrims. Of course, the temples were new to me, not to her. She could visit them anytime; they were in her backyard. We did a small trip to Kanvashram, the ancient ashram of Rishi Kanva on the banks of the Malini River. It is also a place associated with Shakuntala, whom we know better from Kalidasa's play Abhigyan Shakuntalam. In the evening, we visited the ancient Bade Hanumanji Temple. As I was walking around the temple with this gifted lady, she started chanting the Hanuman Chalisa in a low tone. I stood next to her and started chanting along with her. Soon, her voice became normal and we chanted the rest of the Hanuman Chalisa together, took the prasad, and did the *parikrama* of the temple before descending down the steep steps to come back to the car, all in complete silence. A strange comforting connection had been established between us, just by chanting the Hanuman Chalisa together. Then on, I was no longer a guest to be taken around. I was a seeker and she had to contribute to my journey. It was like we were sisters who pray to Hanuman, and this connection continues to stay on till date.

At Beyt Dwarka, the small but significant Dandi Hanuman Temple was closed when I visited. I asked around for its opening time, and as it often happens in India, I got answers ranging from five minutes to an hour. Then I saw a group of people sitting outside the closed saffron door of the temple, chanting the Hanuman Chalisa. I joined in, assuming that the temple would open when the chanting was over. But after one chant cycle, they started another one, then another, and this went on for a while. Initially, I was restless, and with every chant cycle coming to an end, I looked at the door, hoping for it to open. However, after four or five rounds, I was lost in the chant and it really did not matter to me when the door opened. More and more people visiting the temple joined in and I started enjoying this group chant. In just a few minutes, I had started feeling I was a part of the group and not a solo woman visiting the temple.

Meanwhile, as soon as my focus moved inwards and away from the door, it opened. The pujari chastised me when I asked him what the significance of the temple was.

He was flabbergasted. For one, I did not know the importance of the temple, and secondly, I had the guts to ask him about it, straight in the face. He took it upon himself to educate me on the temple. He judged my knowledge of India and Indian scriptures first, before deciding to tell me the story of Hanuman and his son Makardhwaj. I was a rare visitor who did not know this story that connects Beyt Dwarka to Ramayana. Most visitors know the story, while casual visitors do not bother to ask.

The closest example to this feeling of bonding with absolute strangers is what you feel when you suddenly meet a fellow countryman, or someone from your city, in a remote and strange place you are visiting. The common language that you speak among a bunch of strangers in a foreign land can give you that bonding. Spiritual bonding, however, is miles deeper than the bonding of shared homeland, language, or profession. When you realize that the person you just met believes in or prays to the same ishta devata, there is a sibling like emotion that develops almost instantly. When you chant a common *stuti* or a bhajan, you feel a bond that is beyond any definition. Shared poetry and literature too play their own roles. You instantly connect to the person without a need to know anything else about them. It is a kind of trust that does not seek any validation.

Have you felt this unknown connection with people you met on the way? If not, do try to sense it the next time you travel. You may discover human dimensions that you are not even aware but exist right within you. Time and again, I get to encounter such rendezvous which reveal the faith that we nurture beneath a veneer that we wear for the world at large.

Strands of Living Culture

नित्य नूतन, चिर पुरातन।

—Pravasi Panth by Ram Iqbal Singh 'Rakesh'

Eternally old, everyday new.

Our Christian neighbor in Goa comes to our home every Deepawali with a gift for us, and we too visit her with a box of sweets, the same way we visit all our friends. The sequence is repeated on Christmas when we visit her home to wish her. It is one of those perfect scenes that showcase how harmonious life is in India. Last Deepawali, she brought homemade sweets piled on a steel plate. Growing familiarity has slowly let us shed the layers of formality, and thankfully, the enormous wastage by way of packing material. I returned the plate with few other sweets on it. She insisted that our Deepawali sweets had already reached her home, and so there was no need for more sweets. I just shrugged my shoulders and said, "I cannot return the plate empty—take it with sweets or leave it." She laughed out aloud and said, "Oh my God, you too do that!" We then had a short conversation about this tradition being a pan-Indian one—of never returning a vessel empty. She reflected, "We have changed our religion, but these are some of the things we continue to follow from the times we were Hindus." I could see a strange sense of belongingness flash through her expression, a connection she found beyond just being neighbors, a connection that came from following a simple tradition that has its roots somewhere in our common ancient past, irrespective of our differences of the present and the recent past.

India is the oldest continuously living civilization in the world—you hear this said anywhere and everywhere. You get to see glimpses of it in ruined cities, in monuments of the past and in museums. Many scholars comment on the practices and artefacts associated with various Sindhu Saraswati Valley archaeological sites, which continue to be living traditions for many of us, including yoga postures and precursors of some of the deities we worship today. Nevertheless, to stumble upon things that you thought belonged to the past, but are still living in some form or shape today, is like coming face-to-face with a thread from an ancient fabric that has managed to survive, sometimes maintaining a low profile, sometimes lying dormant, and sometimes living on as if nothing has changed. Encountering such living traditions head-on while traveling takes you back in time instantly, and virtually hands you this invisible thread of living traditions of the past.

Mishi Saran in her book 'Chasing the Monk's Shadow', wherein she retraces the footsteps of the seventh century Chinese traveler Huan Tsang, finds many such threads throughout her journey. For instance, somewhere in Andhra Pradesh, she meets a rude beautician in a beauty parlor. She is immediately reminded that this is exactly what the Chinese monk had written about the people of this land, many centuries ago—rude. She finds many typical words that the monk mentioned, associated with the places he wrote about, still in use.

At the Afghan Church in Colaba, Mumbai, I was busy admiring the recessed arches of the beautiful doorway. Someone came quietly and opened the door so that we could go inside. With my eyes fixed on the walls full of stories, I wandered inside the church. The memory of the Afghan war living on in the distant island of Mumbai was fascinating to the history enthusiast in me. The person who had opened the door, came up to me, and asked me sternly, "Why are you wearing shoes inside the church?" I looked around to see if I was the only one doing so. I realized he was the only other person around, and that he was barefoot. I deduced he was the caretaker of the church. My eyes looked around for boards that said, 'No shoes inside the church'. There were none. My mind zoomed back to past visits to churches anywhere on the face of this earth, to recall churches where I had had to take off my shoes. None that I could recall. My thoughts next zipped back to a university hostel conversation, where we had been discussing the pros and cons of visiting temples, mosques, gurudwaras and churches, and one of the points in favor of churches was that you did not have to take off your shoes for entering them. With all this data in my head, I asked him if we are supposed to take off our shoes while visiting the church. He asked me, "Do you take off your shoes when you visit your God?" I said, "Yes, one cannot enter temples with one's shoes on," to which he contended, "Should you not treat the gods of others just like you treat your own God?" He had a point. I pondered over this for a long time. How do we treat deities other than our own? Can we really classify God as mine and not-mine? Practically speaking, when you visit a religious place, should you follow the norms of your tradition or that of the faith whose place you are visiting? For a long time, I quoted this as an example of the wisdom that I gained on the road.

Now, when I look back at this incident through the lens of cultural continuity, I see that the caretaker was carrying forward a tradition from his past, something he did not want to let go. Some gene in his DNA did not permit him to enter a sacred space with his shoes on, even though his faith, a faith he was most probably born into, has no such prescriptions. Somewhere in his subconscious mind, he associated inherent impurity with shoes, and so wanted them to be kept away from the sacred space. This sensibility had to have come from somewhere deep within him, since there was no apparent practice supporting it.

My years in Goa have given me numerous glimpses of the strange ways in which cultural strands refuse to get swept away, and the way they are camouflaged like chameleons in their surroundings, sometimes for survival, and sometimes just to fit into the milieu of the day. One late night, at the beginning of summer, around the festival of Holi or Shigmo as it is celebrated in Goa, I was at Chandor village in South Goa—the ancient capital of Goa. I was there for a festival called Mussel Khel that is unique to this village. Men dressed in colorful attire including traditional headgears, with colorful and decorated bamboo sticks in their hands, go from one end of the road to the other, singing songs and stopping at every home. People wait for them to come to their front yards and sing and dance. The party is offered something before they move on to the next house. At homes that have seen a death in the family in the past one year, only a prayer is said, and no song-and-dance takes place. Now, this village is more or less entirely Christian, and so are the men performing this age-old ritual. Be that as it may, while performing this ritual, they call themselves *kshatriyas*, a generic name for the warrior class among Hindus. Effectively, these villagers are carrying forward the legacy of having been kshatriyas a few generations ago. When I first heard about this, I was immediately reminded of the memoirs of Goan fashion designer Wendell Rodricks, who begins his book by tracing his kshatriya lineage from a village in South Goa.

The songs they sing as they move from house to house recalls Harihara, a brave king of yore and Durga—the patron devi of warrior clans. The path they cover used to begin from an ancient Shiva temple and end at the Maha Shiva Temple at the other end of the road. This ancient Shiva temple lives on through its ruins, with its exposed foundation revealing the floor plan, a giant stone Nandi, and the temple well. Someone lights a lamp at the feet of Nandi even today, though the stone Nandi is broken and technically should not be worshipped. I never got a clear answer as to who lights the lamp every day. Someone does it and chooses to stay anonymous.

Now, of course, the procession of Mussel Khel proceeds from a cross installed next to the stone temple ruins and ends at the chapel at the other end of the road. The priest says a prayer before the ritual begins. I was told this was done by the kshatriya men to assure the villagers that they were there to protect them. Initially, the procession used to happen around Holi, but now it happens alongside the annual carnival, both of which are not too far from each other on the calendar, though the calendar they refer to has changed. Holi is still celebrated based on the lunar calendar followed in India, while the carnival has no fixed date and gets held on any convenient date of the Julian calendar.

There are many scholarly interpretations of these rituals by people on either side. To me though, this is a cultural strand that refuses to go away, that lets the memories of a once-proud kshatriya clan pop up once a year, even if it is just as a fun ritual, and might become a treat for tourists in the future.

Once, in Indonesia, I stayed back after a media trip to explore Bali, to see Bali's Ramayana performances in the evenings and to explore its water temples. Those few days, I was trying to understand Hinduism the way it is followed there. Out of sheer curiosity, I visited many temples, some that are used to having busloads of tourists visiting them, and I was just one them, though perhaps one who spent a little more time than the others. At other temples, I was the only outsider; an outsider because my features did not gel with the crowd and I was not wearing a *sarong*. At places, I tried wearing a sarong to enter the temples, but I was politely refused entry. I tried convincing them that I was a practicing Hindu, but they would hear nothing of it. You are not a Hindu, they said. Beyond a point, as a solo traveler, I gave up, stood in a corner, and tried to observe the rituals. To me, they were following another kind of Hinduism, something that I acknowledged and was trying to understand, having never before seen it in practice. With altars to make offerings, they were probably following something closer to the Vedic culture which I have not seen being followed in India.

Everywhere I went, from shopping malls to high-end hotels to heritage monuments to homes and even temples, I noticed *canag sari* offerings kept for ancestors and deities. On a morning walk, you would find these offerings everywhere—already placed or getting placed. The canag sari is a small basket made by folding a palm leaf, something similar to the prasad baskets you get at the Puri Temple in Odisha, and filled with fruits, flowers, betel leaves and nuts, incense sticks, and sometimes, money. It is a daily ritual that all Balinese Hindus follow, both at their homes and their workplaces. Based on its color, each flower has its placement in a certain direction, as it is directed towards a particular deity. The only time canag saris are not offered is when there is a death in the family.

Now, this was a cultural strand that I had not been aware of; I had never before seen it anywhere nor even read about it. However, some recessive gene inside me did understand it, almost instantaneously. Its presence on every door may have pleasantly surprised me, but I inherently understood the emotion behind the daily ritual. It was the equivalent of the *kolam* in south Indian villages or my own grandmother's tradition of keeping aside a roti each for the cow, dog, and the crow, before we ate ours. It was an offering meant for ancestors, for the spirits that have left us and must not be forgotten. I understood the inherent gratitude in this ritual and if I had to start doing it the next day onwards, I would have happily done so.

On one of those days in Bali, I was returning from a long morning walk, back to Hanoman Road where I was staying. It was a delight to see familiar street names and it constantly reminded me that back home, we do not have streets named after deities or characters from our epics. Anyway, the shops were just being opened. Funky T-shirts were being smartly displayed; some shops were getting cleaned while others were still closed. That was when I heard soft soothing music coming from a shop. I followed the sound and reached a small shop selling, what else, local musical instruments. The glass door was closed, but not locked. The music was getting meditative as I got closer. With a little hesitation, I stepped inside. To my right, a lady in a black T-shirt and a printed black sarong was playing a metallic instrument with her eyes closed in a deep meditative state. It looked as if her hands were on some kind of an auto mode that comes from deep meditation and ample practice. She did not even notice that I had entered the shop.

She was making music from a large metallic inverted bowl with circular grooves in it. Her fingers produced a metallic sound that reverberated in a slight echo, somewhat like a distant temple bell. I could not make out if her tiny eyes were open or closed. Anyway, it would not have mattered, as she was so lost in playing that meditative music that she was oblivious to everything around her. I sat on a bench close by. My eyes closed naturally and after a few minutes, the music stopped. I opened my eyes and exchanged a faint smile with the lady. I sensed that she was used to people getting drawn to her music, and I happened to be that person that day. We spent some quiet moments before she said hello to me while adjusting the instruments around her. I told her that her music had pulled me into the shop. She then played few other instruments to show me how they work.

We started chatting about the instruments. When I told her I was from India, she stopped to look at me. Her eyes suddenly had a sense of longing. With a little hesitation, she asked me if I had been to River Ganga. I said, "Yes, several times." It then occurred to me that I had been in Varanasi just a week before I came to Indonesia. I shared this with her. Reflexively, she asked me, "Have you touched the Ganga?" Yes, I nodded. She instinctively held my hands and asked me to describe the Ganga to her. There were tears in her eyes as I described the Ganga at Kashi and Rishikesh. By touching my hands that had touched the Ganga, she was trying to reach out to the Ganga. We stood holding hands as I narrated my visits to the Ganga.

Ghats of Ganga in Kashi

She said it was her biggest dream to see the Ganga before she died. She had been saving for years so that one day she could visit the Ganga. This was not the dream of a tourist to tick an item off the checklist. This was the longing that comes with faith, from a deep connection with the stories one hears about holy places. It is the longing that takes us on long, arduous pilgrimages.

Slowly, I understood the longing I saw in her eyes when I said India. Nothing that I had ever read about the Ganga or felt at her banks could impress upon me what River

Ganga meant to people, as did this longing in a distant land. This also came as a bit of a surprise, as I had seen so many temples and sculptures all over Bali but could not recall a single Ganga sculpture anywhere. Even though streets here are named after characters like Sugriva and Hanuman, and the walls lined with Bheema and Ghatotkacha murals, it is the Ganga that is longed for.

I do not know if she managed to visit the Ganga or not, but when I was at the Ganga next—during the Kumbh Mela—I prayed for her. I asked Ma Ganga to fulfil her wish, to call her to her banks. I hope my prayers added some weight to her longing.

This incident left a deep impact on me. It opened a window to the deep-rooted connections between India and Indonesia, something—I can say with reasonable authority—that not many of us in India know about. We have no idea of the immensity of what we take for granted; we have no idea that what we choose to ignore is something that others are longing for. At the same time, it connected me at a much deeper level with Bali, as I discovered a shared faith, and a common reverence for the Ramayana as well as for the Ganga.

Earlier, during the same trip, on a remote island in Raja Ampat region that we reached after changing three flights, and thereafter riding a speed boat for a couple of hours, we visited a school and interacted with the students there. I asked the students to tell us what they wanted to become. This question always tells me what the aspirations of that society or community are. One of the common answers that came up was "Guru", the word they use for teacher. I felt I had stepped into another era to hear that word in its right connotation and in the right context. I do not recall hearing that word, in India, to denote teachers who teach you at school or prepare you for life, even though we are all well aware of the word. We have come to label experts as gurus, either in earnestness or as satire.

The same classroom also taught me that the threads of the 21st century that united the young students of this island with India were Bollywood songs. In a place where not a single word of Hindi is spoken or understood, young girls could sing complete songs of Arijit Singh without missing a note and without mispronouncing a word. If today, it is the Internet that lets these connections happen, I wonder what was the glue that connected us ages ago, and who or what were the carriers of cultures in the past.

Sometime back, I was reading Meenakshi Jain's book 'Flight of Deities and Rebirth of Temples', wherein she mentions a story from Kalhana's Rajatarangini that dates back to the 12th century and is considered the most authoritative text on Kashmir's history and genealogy. In it, Kalhana talks about how King Lalitaditya, who ruled during the eighth century, discovered a lost temple when he encountered two young maidens singing and dancing on a wasteland, every day, and even took a bow on that spot before returning home, in Suravardhamana village. Upon inquiry, he discovered that they were dancing girls of temples, who were keeping alive the dance tradition of the temple they belonged to, a tradition handed down to them. They knew nothing more than this. The wise king got the ground the girls were dancing upon dug up and discovered two dilapidated temples and two murtis there! An inscription indicated that the murtis were that of Ram and Lakshman. Lalitaditya got the murtis shifted to Parihasapur, about twenty-two kilometers from Srinagar, and had separate temples built for them. This incident told me two things—one, you never know how many untold, unexplained traditions you may be carrying intuitively from your preceding generations. At some point in time, when the time is right, the package will be opened, analyzed, rediscovered, and if need be, revived. Second, it tells me that temples fell into misuse or disuse even way before the eighth century. The most amazing message of this story is how a society may preserve its traditions even when everything is seemingly lost, and because the tradition has been preserved, what is considered lost may be recovered and revived.

In Marcel, a remote Goan village, one day, during the peak of the monsoon season, a literal riot takes place in the mud. It is probably the oldest living mud festival in the world. On the grounds of the Devaki Krishna Temple of the village, all the menfolk of the village can be seen rolling in mud and playing games. It is believed that when Devaki met Krishna after many years, she could not recognize him as she had seen him only as an infant. So, Krishna reverted to his childhood form as Bal Krishna, so that his mother could hold him in her arms. That moment is frozen in the murti in this temple. On the 12th day of the month of Ashadh, that roughly falls in mid-July, all the males in the village—right from toddlers to senior citizens—become Bal Krishnas. They play the same games that Krishna used to play in Braj. They roll in the mud, throw mud on each other, and play games like *mendrani*—a sheep and wolf game, *chakra* game in which the formation of a chakra is made, blind man game in which a blindfolded man has to listen to cymbals and follow the sound, *dharchyani* game similar to dog and the bone game, tug of war, and tunnel game (which some attempt to escape from), among other games. In the end, everyone is divided into two groups and a wedding scene is enacted with one of the groups representing the bride's side and the other group the groom's side. There is a war of words that leaves everyone in splits. The festival culminates with the favorite sport of Bal Krishna, the stealing of butter, for which the young boys create a pyramid to reach a *dahi handi* tied high up on a tree. Their oiled bodies covered with mud now carry a layer of curd and they are ready to visit the *dhobi talao* or the washermen's quarters, where they will be given a ritual bath. On this day, early in the morning, the boys would have visited the village grocery store, and the grocer would have applied oil on each of them, his shop lined with cans of oil for applying on the Bal Krishnas of the day. When I asked the shopkeeper who sponsored it, he said, "This is my *adhikar* or right, which I have inherited from my ancestors—to apply oil on Krishna. It is my seva, I will not let anyone else sponsor it." On the day of this festival, elderly men go around placing cotton in the ears of young boys. Women go around distributing homemade sweets piled in a basket—*puran poli*, jalebi, laddus. There is no commerce, just the joint celebration of an age-old festival. It is one of the most pure and unadulterated festivals I have ever seen. You have to see it to understand what fun playing in mud can be.

After witnessing this mud festival, I was spending some time in Braj. As I walked the parikrama path around the Govardhan Parvat, most of which is a mud path, I kept hearing "*Braj ki raj*" meaning "The dust of Braj is supreme." It is believed that the dust here is charged with the presence of Radha and Krishna. Almost everyone in Braj will tell you that only three things remain in Braj since the time of Krishna—River Yamuna, Govardhan Parvat and Braj ki raj. There are anecdotes of people coming to roll in the dust of Braj, to become one with the soil that was once the ground where Krishna played. Leave alone devotees, there are even stories of other pilgrimage places visiting Braj to partake its dust to wash away all the sins they had accumulated from the pilgrims who had come to them to wash away their sins! There are stories of rich merchants wanting their dead bodies to be dragged in the dust of Braj so that they become one with it. Aren't the people of Marcel village in Goa similarly celebrating dust in their own way? Are they creating their own little Braj at a temple dedicated to the little Krishna of Braj? How this tradition reached this coastal hamlet from far-away Braj is something that needs to be studied, but to me, this is another strand of culture that has potentially moved from one region to another and survived. Did it travel along with ancient travelers who settled there? Did someone from Goa travel to Braj and bring home this tradition? I must add here that Goa is primarily a Shiva-Shakti dominated place, and most ancient temples here are dedicated to them. There are not too many Vishnu temples or temples dedicated to Ram and Krishna. This temple is almost an exception. Incidentally, this temple was earlier located on the island of Chorao on the Mandovi River, which was originally called the Gomti. It was moved to this hinterland village during Portuguese rule.

Speaking of the Portuguese, I was at the Thiruketeshwara Temple in Mannar, Sri Lanka, to do a story on the ongoing construction at the temple. This is an ancient Shiva temple, believed to have been built by Ketu of the Rahu-Ketu duo, and it stands at the other end of the Ram Setu. So, if the Indian end of the Ram Setu has the Rameshwaram Temple, the Sri Lankan end has the Thiruketeshwara Temple. Mannar is an ancient port town that has seen a golden age but is now a small dusty coastal town. This temple is fairly large when seen in the backdrop of the town of Mannar but is nothing compared to how it used to be in its hay days. While reading up on the history of the temple, I discovered the contribution of the Pandya and Chola kings to the temple. The temple was completely erased from the landscape of Mannar during the Portuguese days. Its memories too went into oblivion until a young man found a description of the temple in ancient Tamil poetry and went on a mad hunt to rediscover the temple. A long struggle culminated in unearthing of evidence of the temple, including a Chola era Shivalinga, and further led to the rebuilding of the lost temple. The new Shivalinga had to be installed and it came all the way from Kashi via the Rameshwaram Temple. When I stood before this Shivalinga that had been carved in Kashi, and hence revered all the more in an ancient temple in Sri Lanka, I saw a small cultural thread connecting the two ancient lands. A connection that may have been severed several times since the days of the Ramayana, but something that is renewed every now and then.

Later, during another travel, at the Omkareshwar Temple in Madikeri town of the Coorg region of Karnataka, I would see another Shivalinga that had been brought from Kashi by the local king. I wonder if there are many more Shiva temples where Shivalingas have been brought from Kashi, the city of Shiva, or if these are a rarity. The search is on.

Strands of living culture can also be seen on stone sculptures that have managed to live to tell the stories. For example, in the temples of Kanchipuram, anyone who understands even a little about the architectural styles of major south Indian dynasties like the Pallavas, Cholas, Pandyas and the Vijayanagara empire, can succinctly tell you which parts were built by whom. There are signature elements of these dynasties that can be seen on the parts of the temples they had built or renovated. The pillars with a lion at the base are from the Pallava period, and these can be seen in the oldest temples of the city. At the Vaikuntha Perumal Temple, you see some of the lion-base pillars repaired at a later date by the Vijayanagara rulers; the color of the stone used has changed, the style of sculpting of the lions at the base of the pillars has changed, but overall, the style has been maintained. A trained eye would be able to see many such nuances that narrate the story of how these temples were maintained by successive generations of rulers, and the fact that successive dynasties ruling these cities respected the deities in these temples.

The prehistoric paintings of Bhimbetka show layers and layers of paintings one over the other. These are indications of both a constant renewal and a continued tradition. The same space was used to paint new scenes every now and then, probably as part of some ritual, just like how, even today in rural India, ritual paintings are done for select annual festivals or during family events like weddings. The Madhubani paintings of Mithila, Warli paintings of Dadra, and the Gond paintings of Central India are all connected to prehistoric rock art though an invisible thread.

Chola bronzes are the most exquisite metal art that India has ever produced. The perfect body proportions and the right bends and swells make them as humanlike as metal can get. Most of these were *utsav murtis,* the murtis that represent the deity in the sanctum of the temple and move outside the sanctum too. These are the deities that step out to meet devotees, take a tour of their *kshetras,* or go on a boat ride. My interest in Chola bronzes was first triggered when I saw the giant Nataraja on display at the National Museum in New Delhi. Later, I would see many of them at Thanjavur, and visit the Egmore Museum in Chennai just to see its exquisite collection of Chola bronzes. There, I saw a film on the making of metalcraft using the ancient lost wax casting method. Each piece is first made with wax, which is then covered with clay in such a way that the clay takes its shape. The clay mould is then heated and the wax allowed to flow out. It leaves an empty mould into which the molten metal is poured and left to take the shape of the mould. Once it cools down, the clay mould is broken to reveal the shining metal replica of the wax model. There is no scope of rectifying any mistake made in crafting the wax model. I watched the film and was in complete awe of the artisans who worked with this method. It is said that the process is at least five thousand years old. I wondered if in some corner of India, someone still used this process. My limited knowledge of the world said that even if it was being used, it would be at some elite art studio, by someone attempting to revive or experiment with this method. Well, I could not have been more wrong.

Dokra Artist with her creation

About fifteen hundred kilometers north of Chennai, in a small village called Ektal in the remote regions of Chhattisgarh, I found the 21st century home of this metal art. The entire village is involved in making bronze art using the lost wax method. Here, you not only see metal being crafted into beautiful pieces of all sizes and shapes, you also get to understand how art clusters would have worked in the past. All families in the village, and most family members within each family, are involved in creating these masterpieces. I sat and saw the women creating delicate wax models, while the men worked at pressing wax into strips, heating the clay mould and then breaking them. All over the village, clay moulds stuffed with wax designs were waiting to be baked. It was like reliving the film I had seen some time back in Chennai. Who would have thought that this ancient form continues to live in a remote hinterland of India? At Ektal, they were making mostly murtis of deities, folk deities, folk tale characters and bronze toys. They proudly showed me their national award-winning exquisite creations. I wondered if this metalcraft would see some innovation, or if it would stay true to the inherited tradition.

Well, I had to travel about six hundred kilometers north-east of Ektal, to Bishnupur in Bengal, to see lovely contemporary jewelry getting crafted in yellow metal using the same lost wax method. I immediately bought some. Every time I wear it, it feels like wearing an age-old tradition that may have gone out of sight and hence out of mind, but had never really left this land. Imagine wearing something made in exactly the same way the 'Dancing girl of Harappa' was made in the Sindhu Saraswati Civilization that we are still trying to date!

A similar story unfolded when I visited the world's oldest known port at Lothal in Gujarat. The museum on the site displays micro beads in white color that are so minute that one needs a magnifying glass to see them. What technology did those ancestors of ours have to create such microscopic beads? Where and for what purpose were these beads used for? Later, I would meet the descendants of these people in Jhabua district of Madhya Pradesh, not too far from Gujarat. There, I saw handmade jewelry made with similar micro beads in vibrant colors. The only difference was the material used—nowadays it is plastic—and that the beads are machine-made.

"Sonu loves Pinky" kind of graffiti troubles us when we see it etched on the walls of heritage monuments. It pains us when we see them on the paintings of Ajanta, or the walls of an ancient monument, or on the trunks of age-old trees. I often speak out against this disgusting habit of ours to imprint our names on our heritage spaces. It feels as if these modern-day lovers are defiling the sanctity of the ancient spaces. That was until I came across the Jogimara Cave inscription in the remote jungles of the Ramgarh Hills in Chhattisgarh, better known for being a 'Kalidasa's Natyashala' or a naturally formed amphitheater. The inscription is a similar claim of love by a sculptor named Devadinna for a devadasi named Sutanuka. This is the earliest known graffiti on a rock face. Many of the caves in Chhattisgarh have pre-historic rock paintings and our sculptor friend may well have defaced some earlier-painted story to announce his love. Connecting the dots, it seems, we are just carrying forward a long-standing tradition of imprinting our names wherever we think it would remain long after we are gone.

Another thing that used to bother me a lot was the inscribing of names of donors on marble tiles, in temples. In some temples, it is difficult to find a single empty tile. All of them are full of donor names who have contributed to the temple. They typically mention the name of the donor, the amount donated, the reason for the donation—which usually is in memory of a parent or grandparent or a relative—and the name of the place the donor is from. You mostly see names of ancestral towns, rather than the big cities where the families have probably moved to. As a kid, I wondered, what was the need to mention names? Shouldn't the donation be anonymous? Is a temple the right place to announce one's philanthropy? Don't we say that we should do charity in such a way that when one hand gives, even the other hand should not get to know of it? This was until I read about and visited Buddhist sites like the Sanchi Stupa. These sites are full of mentions of donations made by all kinds of people—kings, traders, Buddhist *bhikkus, bhikunis,* commoners, and *sethis* or merchants. Their names, the names of their family members, the places they come from, and sometimes, the purpose of donation finds mention here. Much of what we know about the socio-economic status of the society of those days is from these donation inscriptions. The copper plate inscriptions—the official records of grants made by the state for the religious institutions—is another source that helps. The aesthetics of these donation inscriptions on stone is better than the aesthetics of donation inscriptions on the ceramic or marble tiles of today, but then, who knows what they looked like when the stone may not have been bare as we see it now. This then, is another strand with a history going back to at least two millennia.

I can go on with many more examples, but I hope these are enough to trigger thoughts on the way culture manages to stay alive across generations. Sometimes, I wonder, are we all carrying some strands within us that connect us to our distant past? Do these strands have the intelligence to show up at the right time, or do we need to train our eyes, hearts, and minds to be able to discern them? I am still trying to find answers to these questions, even while encountering new strands every other day.

Warp and Weft of Shared Stories

पुण्या कनखले गंगा कुरुक्षेत्रे सरस्वती ।
ग्रामे वा यदि वारण्ये पुण्या सर्वत्र नर्मदा ॥

—Padma Puran

Ganga is holy in Haridwar, Saraswati in Kurukshetra, but Narmada is holy in every village and forest she touches.

"You have reached just the right place. You can go to every *tirtha,* but your pilgrimage, your yatra, is not complete until you come to Narmada ji," said a purohit, as he performed the rituals for the Narmada puja on her ghats at Omkareshwar. I have heard such adulation in almost every pilgrimage site across India. People living on the banks of the Narmada believe she is the prime river of India, to the people living on the banks of the Yamuna, the Yamuna is the empress, so too is the Kaveri to the people she nurtures, even though they all continue to invoke the Ganga in their daily prayers.

There are some stories that I have heard again and again across the length and breadth of India. No matter where I traveled, I encountered these stories in some form and shape. Every time I sat down to listen, these stories were told in a manner that proclaimed that all rights to the stories rested with those particular places, and that the events of the story happened only there and nowhere else.

Initially, as a naïve traveler, I would try to tell people that I had heard these stories and claims elsewhere too. Citing examples, I would narrate anecdotes from my earlier travels. Without exception, people would instantly get offended, sometimes going to the extent of fighting with me or ridiculing me for my stand. However, over time, I have learnt to respect the faith that people have in their own versions of the stories and their belief that the story belongs to them and to them alone. Now, with crumbs of wisdom collected along the way, when I encounter these stories, I sit back and listen with ample curiosity and awe, as if I am hearing them for the first time. Over time, I have also realized that stories, like life, happen in the moment; so if someone tells you that you are standing at the ultimate tirtha, that is the truth of that moment. Your past and future pilgrimages belong to a different time and space. The biggest tirtha, and the most sacred of them all, is the one that you are present in, at this moment.

Was this how our ancestors felt when they were on pilgrimages? Did the walls of our temples and public spaces tell them the same stories again and again, like reminders from the past? Are these stories repeated reminders to tell us that we belong to the same past and are descendants of the same ancestors? Are these the lessons that history preserved for us, so that we do not repeat their mistakes?

India can well be called a land of stories and storytellers – you find them written in stone, on walls, on rocks, as weaves and on palm leaves, though none of them beat the oral rendition through the innumerable storytelling traditions across the land. There are some stories that are so entwined in the DNA of an Indian soul that no matter where you start from, you somehow end up at these stories from a distant past. At times, the stories span the geography of India, and at times, they travel all around like a performing troupe, with minor adjustments suited to the place they are in

Sati: Marking the Sacred Geography of India

Sati is one of the twenty-four daughters of Daksha Prajapati and his wife Prasuti. Thirteen of the daughters—Shraddha, Lakshmi, Dhriti, Pushti, Tushti, Medha, Kriya, Budhhi, Lajja, Vapu, Shanti, Siddhi and Kirti—were married to Dharma. The other ten—Khyati, Sambhuti, Smriti, Priti, Kshama, Sannati, Anusuya, Urja, Swaha and Swadha—married Bhrigu, Marichi, Angira, Pulatsya, Pulah, Kratu, Atri, Vasishth, Agni and Pitra, respectively. One daughter, Sati, is adamant on marrying Shiva. Shiva being an ascetic with no material wealth—something that any father looks for in a potential groom for his daughter—was not Daksha's choice for Sati. There is a disagreement between the father and the daughter. Ultimately, rebellious Sati goes ahead and marries Shiva and lives happily with him in the Kailash Parvat or the Mount Kailash range of the Himalayas.

From her abode on the Gandhmadan Hill, one day, Sati watches everyone marching towards Kankhal, her father's home, dressed in their best finery, including Indra with Shachi, and the moon or Chandra with Rohini and his other wives. She sends her friends to enquire as to what was happening, and learns that her father Daksha was performing a great yagna, for which he had invited every sage and every devata—including even the minor ones like *lokpals, gandharvas* and *kinnars.* He has invited everyone of consequence, except her husband Shiva. Now Indian tradition holds the son-in-law in an exalted position; he is considered equivalent to a devata and is treated as the most important guest in any family gathering or event.

At the *yagna shala* at Kankhal or Gangadwar, as Haridwar was then known, in the middle of the proceedings, Rishi Dadhichi advised Daksha Prajapati to reach out to Shiva and invite him, as no auspicious endeavor can be complete without his presence—both as the supreme deity, as well as a son-in-law of the house. However, Daksha had an old axe to grind with Shiva, as the latter had ignored him in the forests of Naimisharanya in front of all the learned rishis there. Daksha remembered this insult and was firm on retaliating to it by not inviting Shiva to this most important yagna that he was conducting. Rishi Dadhichi left the yagna shala after advising Daksha in vain, as Dakhsa chose to ignore him too.

Sati, torn between the happenings at her father's place and her husband's pride, decides to go to the yagna shala and question her father. Shiva tries to dissuade her, but when has a man been able to stop a woman from doing something that she has decided to do? Shiva knows he would be losing her in the process and may never see her again in the same form as Sati, his beloved wife. Eventually, he lets her go, sending his dependable Nandi and other Ganas with her. Sati reaches Kankhal and questions her father, who has nothing but insults for the son-in-law who does not fit into the galaxy of well-dressed and well-presented celestial beings from all over. He says, "What does Shiva know of the world of kings? He only knows how to live in the cremation ground with ash covering his body." Sati is unable to take this insult to her husband, or to go back to her husband after this insult. She decides to jump into the yagna fire, immolating herself. The Shiva Ganas go on a rampage. One of them heads to Shiva and informs him of Sati's death. Shiva creates Veerbhadra from the locks of his hair and lets him lead the destruction at Daksha's yagna. Shiva then holds the charred body of Sati in his arms and performs *tandava*—the dance of destruction. Vishnu realizes this would cause absolute destruction of the universe and must be stopped. He starts chopping the dead body of Sati with his Sudarshan Chakra. They fall at different places, sanctifying the place where they fall. All these places would become sacred as the Shaktipeethas and evoke remembrance of the incident forever. I will come back to the Shaktipeethas in the chapter on the Devi.

The story of Sati is at the core of every tradition as it involves Shiva, Shakti, and Vishnu—all the three major deities worshipped by Hindus. It is essayed in many scriptures; you can hear it in every Shakta temple, and from every follower of the Shiva-Shakti tradition. I have heard it many times at many temples and tirthas, but when this story came alive for me was when I visited the Daksheshwar Mahadev Temple in Kankhal—the oldest living part of Haridwar on the banks of the Ganga. This is believed to be the place where Daksha's yagna took place, where Sati had immolated herself. A yagna *kund* is at the heart of this temple. The temple was set up by Daksha once he was resurrected with the head of a goat by Shiva.

Somewhere between Haridwar and Rishikesh is a small village called Veerbhadra. I have spent many of my summer vacations in this village, which has a public sector township where my uncle used to work. However, I never associated it with the Sati story. I was not even aware of the role of Veerbhadra in the story. I never questioned where the word Veerbhadra came from; it was just a place, a summer holiday destination, a favorite *bua's* home.

It was during one of my study trips to Haridwar that I came to know that there was an ancient Veerbhadra temple located there, which lends the village its name. The temple is small but practicing. It resembles the other hill temples of Shiva, especially the Kedarnath Temple. When I visited the temple, I somehow felt that this may not be the original temple of Veerbhadra. I asked around and sure enough, I was led to the stone ruins of an ancient Veerbhadra temple. All we can see there now is the base of the temple and some excavated remains. I assume the important excavated material is with ASI in some museum vault.

Today, the Kankhal temple and the Veerbhadra temple are about twenty-five kilometers apart, but both are by the banks of the Ganga. I wonder if Daksha's yagna grounds had extended all across this distance, which is not surprising, if you read the description of the elaborate gathering at Daksha's yagna. From my reading of the Skanda Puran and the Padma Puran, it looks like all of divinity descended here for the yagna.

On another occasion, I was at the Kopeshwar Mahadeva Temple in Khidrapur village on the Maharashtra-Karnataka border, not too far from Kolhapur. I was there as I had heard a lot about the unique open-to-sky architecture of this temple along with some finely carved masterpieces of the Badami Chalukyans, especially the exquisite Madanikas that are seen even inside the garbhagriha or the sanctum sanctorum of the temple. The temple is stunning and beautiful even in its ravaged state. The open-to-sky swarga mandapa leaves you thinking about the architectural genius that has been recessive in our genes for many centuries now. I had visited this temple during the peak summer months and the purohit had been busy doing a *dahi bhat abhishek* of the main Shivalinga. There are two Lingas here, one representing Shiva and the other representing Vishnu. I saw the purohit painstakingly place layers of milky white curd and rice on the black stone of the Shivalinga, creating a human-like face with black ink on it, and carve out a small Ganapati on the side. Standing next to it, I felt as if I was being cooled down by the paste. The purohit told me that indeed, this paste was applied every day during the summer months to keep Shiva cool. How did this strange practice come to be? Well, that is the story of this temple.

This temple marks the moment in time when Sati has immolated herself at Daksha's yagna; Nandi and Veerbhadra are there at the yagna, and Vishnu is standing next to Shiva, trying his best to alleviate Shiva's anger that could destroy the universe. It is just after this moment that Shiva would do his tandava dance holding the charred body of Sati in his arms, and Vishnu would use his Sudarshan Chakra to cut it into pieces, which would scatter her body uniformly across the geography of India, making it a sacred geography sanctified by the presence of the Devi herself.

As I listened to this story, my guide Shashank pointed out that there was no Nandi or Nandi mandapa in this temple, as this temple denotes the moment when Nandi has accompanied Sati to the yagna, and so he cannot be there with Shiva. I wondered if the open-to-sky architecture too had some relevance to the story, as it is here that Shiva would rise and dance. Most experts opine that the open-to-sky was to let out the smoke emanating from yagna to leave freely. My sense is that there is more to it, as yagna shalas are routinely found in temples, and are either in the open or have a regular roof over them; they are never in open-to-sky mandapas. I would later learn that on Kartik Purnima, a fortnight after the festival of Deepawali, the full moon is aligned to this circular opening and illuminates the mandapa below. The moon as we know sits on the forehead of Shiva. So, this temple's story still has some windows waiting to be opened.

Churning of the Ocean

If you have departed from Bangkok's Suvarnabhumi Airport in the last few years, you have probably seen its large public art installation that looks like a tug of war. This is the biggest tribute that I know of, to one of the oldest known stories of the world. This story finds a mention in many ancient Indian scriptures including the Vishnu Puran, Bhagwat Puran, and the epic Mahabharata. It is the story of Amrita Manthan—the churning of the ocean for the amrita or nectar of immortality. The devas and asuras were at war and the asuras led by Bali had won over the devas and began to rule the universe. As always, the devas approached Vishnu to manage the situation for them. He advised them to churn the ocean—along with the asuras—to access and partake the amrita that would emerge from it, on the agreement of dividing it equally between them and the asuras. The actual plan was to acquire the amrita for just the devas so that they become immortal and live forever to rule the universe.

Churning of the ocean was a huge task and needed an appropriately huge churning rod. Mount Mandar or Mandar Parvat was chosen as the rod. Serpent Nag Vasuki was chosen as the rope to churn the ocean. *Kurma* or the turtle avatar of Vishnu became the platform to support the Mandar Parvat, to prevent it from getting submerged in the ocean. The churning brings out many things from the ocean before the desired amrita emerged, precisely as in life, how we encounter good and bad things along the way on our journey to our final goal or destination. Of these finds, Vishnu received Devi Lakshmi who came out of the ocean and chose to be his consort; other things to emerge included the precious gemstone called Kaustubh Mani and the divine bow named Sharanga. Kamdhenu—the wish fulfilling cow emerged, and Brahma handed her over to the sages to ensure an unending supply of milk and milk products for them. Indra, the leader of the devas received Airavata, a white elephant, and the flowering parijata tree, to take to his Indraloka. Uchhaishrava—the seven-headed horse was taken by Bali, the leader of the asuras. Shiva received the moon that he wears on his forehead. More famously, Shiva receives the Halahal poison that no one is willing to take. He drinks it and holds the poison in his throat, which turns his throat blue, earning him the name Neelkanth.

Finally, Dhanvantari, the father of ayurveda, emerges with a pot of nectar in his hands. The devas and the asuras now start fighting over it. Vishnu's vehicle Garuda flies away with the pot of nectar to secure it for the Devas. In the meantime, Vishnu takes his enchantress form of Mohini to distract the asuras and starts distributing the amrita. An asura disguises himself as a deva and partakes the amrita. Using his Sudarshan Chakra, Vishnu instantly cuts the asura into two pieces, but now that the asura has consumed the nectar, he is immortal, and the two parts of his body become what we know as Rahu and Ketu, Rahu being the asura's head and Ketu his headless body. It is believed that with this, the war ended, and the devas got their reign back—justified or not, we can debate for generations to come.

It is believed that four drops of the same nectar fell on four locations—Haridwar, Prayag, Ujjain and Nashik. Now, the story of how exactly these drops fall has many versions. In one version, the person carrying the pot kept it at these four places; in another, the drops fell when Garuda was flying with the pot. However, the places where the drops fall remain the same in all versions, and always on the banks of a holy river—the Ganga as she enters the plains from the Himalayas at Haridwar, the confluence or Sangam of the Ganga, Yamuna and Saraswati at Prayag, at the origin of the Godavari in Nashik, and on the banks of River Kshipra in Ujjain. All the four places are venues for the once-in-twelve years fairs or melas that are generically called the Kumbh Melas. The mela at Nashik and Ujjain are actually called Simhastha, as they happen When Jupiter is in the Simha Rashi or Zodiac Sign of Leo. The one at Prayag should actually be called Makarasth as it happens when the Sun is in Makar Rashi or Capricorn. The one at Haridwar is truly the Kumbh Mela, and using the same logic, some scholars conclude that of the four places, this may be the original or the oldest venue of the mela.

You encounter the story of Samudra Manthan at all these four places. People in these places feel special as drops of nectar fell there, as if to add sacred sanctity to them forever. The rivers here are believed to wash away all the sins of those who take a dip in them, especially during these auspicious celestial configurations that reoccur every twelve years. When I visited the Kumbh Mela at Prayag, the whole city was decorated with imagery from this story—all the things that came out of the ocean were painted and recreated all over the city. It was like a reminder of the divine origin of the tradition that has been going on unhindered since then.

In the far south, in the town of Kumbakonam in Tamil Nadu, a Kumbh Mela takes place every twelve years, pretty much like the Kumbh Melas of the four locations in the North. I am sure you noticed that the name of the city itself contains the word *kumbha,* that means a pot. Godavari Pushkaram is a similar, once-in-twelve years congregation that takes place on the banks of the Godavari in Telangana and Andhra Pradesh. River Godavari flows eastwards from Nashik to reach the Bay of Bengal. Though this mela happens along the entire stretch of the river and not at a particular point like the four Kumbh Melas of the north, making this a distributed event, the concept remains the same.

I have already mentioned of my own experience of the Kumbh Mela that it feels surreal that somehow, everyone just turns up to participate in the mela. Every time I think of this synchronized movement of people from across the country, I am fascinated by the precise spatio-temporal projections or forecasts of the planets, nakshatras and *tithis* available in the Indian calendar, which we call the panchang. These are universally available in every town and village of Bharat, and you would find them hanging in most homes. You will even find the localized versions that tell you the exact movements of planets, times of sunrise, sunset, moonrise, moonset, etc., based on the precise latitude and longitude of your town. People like me carry the panchang in the form of mobile apps that serve the same purpose. It suddenly made me aware of the fact that our ancestors, even thousands of years ago, knew how to precisely read the skies, calculate the movements of celestial bodies and design calendars based on them. It made me question the science I was taught at school, that claimed that we started discovering the solar system and other celestial objects after the telescope was discovered. Is there a disconnect between our ancient knowledge and its availability to people at large? Not really, since a common Indian can and does read the panchang, and has been acting precisely according to it, all along. Today, though we follow the universal Julian calendar for our day-to-day life and official work, we still manage to follow the panchang for our annual festivals, as well as for our personal rituals like weddings and for calculating the right *muhurat* or auspicious time to start significant initiatives in life.

Are we still reinventing the wheel by not looking at the ocean of knowledge that is present in our civilizational heritage? Were the languages that our ancestors spoke different from the ones we understand now? Can there be a mapping to unearth the knowledge and the techniques that our ancestors have already discovered or invented, so that we can start building from there? These are some of the questions that I am still struggling with.

Paying Heed to the Cows

We know that over a long period of time, scores of Hindu temples were destroyed, desecrated and broken by invaders who did not believe in murti puja. Most of the time, the main deity was taken away from the temple to save it from desecration and destruction. The main murti of the presiding deity of the temple is also the soul of the temple, and a living being once the *pran pratishtha* or installation is done. When invaders were at large, purohits, villagers and devotees took the deities away, and hid them wherever they could. Rich ones would keep them in their palatial homes, but most of the time, even their homes were under attack. Scores of deities were kept in water bodies like wells or temple tanks or village ponds, and they remained hidden underwater. Sometimes, pits were dug to hide the deities underground. Some of these people who hid the deities may have returned and retrieved them, but many of them never came back. Some of them may have never found an opportune moment in their lifetime to retrieve the deities, or not have had access to an appropriate temple to relocate them. Generations would have passed, and the deities would have stayed hidden in their hideouts. These hidden deities keep emerging at different points in time. Each re-emergence is a story in itself, which we hear in different temples across India. Now, whether you think this to be coincidental or divinely ordained is your choice.

One of the common stories that I have heard involves cows coming to a particular spot to drain their milk. These stories go like this: The cowherd finds the cow missing on his way back home or that there is no milk left in her for her own calf or for the milkman. He decides to follow the cow for the next few days, and that is when he witnesses this miracle—that the cow voluntarily drains her milk at a particular spot every day. He shares this with the village elders and they decide to dig up the place. Deities—most of the time a Shivalinga, but sometimes, other deities too—emerge from the spot. Now seen as a *swayambhu* or self-manifested murti, the deity—or deities, as the case may be—are reinstalled in a temple and regular worship resumes for them. The cowherd gets due place in this temple as a minor deity, and the right for his community to keep supplying milk to the deities.

It is said that King Vikramaditya rediscovered Ayodhya in this manner and rebuilt it from scratch, around two thousand years ago. During my own travels, I heard a similar story at the Mangueshi Temple in Goa. The original temple was located in the village of Kushasthali—now called Cortalim—on the banks of River Aghnashini, now called the Zuari River. During Portuguese rule, the temple was destroyed, and no one really knows where the deity was moved to. Once, a villager called Mulki noticed that one of his cows was not giving milk, and that she went missing every evening. He followed the cow and found her draining all her milk over a stone. When the place was dug, a huge Shivalinga in black stone was discovered. This is now at the garbhagriha of a new temple at Priol village in the hinterlands of Goa. A small temple dedicated to Mulki, now called Shri Mulkeshwar stands beside the main temple, and every visitor pays his respects to him, as Shiva had chosen to reveal himself to Mulki. Some other legends say that, originally, the Shivalinga had been brought to Bihar by the Bhagirathi River from her source in the Himalayas, and thereafter had reached Goa along with the Saraswat Brahmin families who arrived there. How fascinating is the journey of our deities!

In a variation of the same story, someone gets a dream that the deity remains hidden somewhere and wants to be reinstalled. I heard this story at the Charbhuja Temple in Merta, the native village of poet-saint Mirabai in Rajasthan. In this variation, the cow belonged to a person from the cobbler community, and this community continues to supply milk for the deity at the Charbhuja Temple till date. Additionally, Rao Duda, the grandfather of Mirabai gets a dream that the four-armed Vishnu is awaiting a temple to be built for him, when this cow spots this beautiful four-armed murti of Vishnu in black stone. The glass murals on the temple walls picture the story of the rediscovery of the Vishnu murti.

At the Khatu Shyam Temple, the murti believed to be the head of Khatu Shyam or Barbarik—grandson of Bheema in Mahabharata—was found in a similar fashion, way back in the 11th century, when a cow was found giving milk at a spot. This spot is now known as the Shyam Kund, and it is one of the most venerated places in the village, along with the temple. The murti was handed over to the purohits, and the then ruler, Roop Singh Chauhan, built a temple for the murti. Legend also has it that Roop Singh Chauhan received the order to build this temple in his dream. As per other records, it was his queen, Narmada, who dreamt of Khatu Shyam appearing in their kingdom and asking for a temple. He is now worshipped as the kul devata by many Rajput Chauhan families.

I heard a slightly different version of this story at Nandiwade village near the coastal town of Ganpatiphule in Maharashtra. There is an ancient Shiva temple, that seems to almost hang out from a cliff close to Jaigad fort. Sea waves constantly pound the rockface on which the temple stands. You can feel the force of these waves when you stand on the cliff close to the temple. It is said that a Shivalinga used to be washed ashore by the waves. Every time this happened, the fishermen would return the Shivalinga back to the sea. Adamant, the Shivalinga kept coming back, sometimes carried by the sea waves, and sometimes in the fishing nets of the fishermen. Finally, one day, the fishermen left it on this cliff. Cows in the area started visiting the Shivalinga and bathing it with their milk. This is when the villagers gathered that it was no ordinary stone or Shivalinga that had chosen to live in their village. A temple was built around the Shivalinga, and the Shivalinga continues to be worshipped. When I asked when this happened, the only answer I got was, "Long, long ago."

Has this story of cows rediscovering hidden murtis traveled across India, or has it recurred at all these places? This is a matter to be studied. Some of the other questions these retellings across the country left me with are: Is it possible that cows can sense the energy field of deities that have been worshipped for centuries? Is it possible that the ancestors of these cows have served milk to these deities through devotees, especially the Shivalingas, which are regularly offered milk abhishek at temples, both by purohits as well as by devotees? Is it possible that some DNA memory takes these cows to the places where these deities are lying hidden beneath the earth's surface or underwater? Could this sensitivity be one of the many reasons we treat cows with so much reverence? Is there a pattern here that we are yet to decipher?

Deity's Choice

While we may think that we build temples for deities, that

it is we who choose the place they would be located in, how big or small they would be, what kind of material the temple would be built with, and what style of architecture the temple would follow, there are stories that repeatedly tell us that it is the deities who choose all this for themselves. You can make whatever plans you wish for them, but they can get adamant like a child, and secure what they want. Again, stories of deities themselves choosing the places they wish to live in come from across the country, with some variations here and there.

The Dadabari Jain temple is a big and beautiful Jain temple located in Mehrauli, the oldest living locality of Delhi. A big board on the Mehrauli-Gurgaon Road announces it, but not many people take the small detour from this busy road to explore it. I visited the temple a couple of times and discovered this fascinating piece of Delhi's Jain history. The 13th century Jain muni, Dada Shri Jinchandra Suri hailed from Jaisalmer and was called Manidhari as he was born with a *mani* or a precious gemstone on his forehead. He was a child prodigy who took *deeksha* at the age of six, and by the time he was nine, he was an *acharya*. He was told by his guru to not enter Delhi, as it would mean death for him. However, a royal order from the then king, Madanpal, brought him to Delhi where he built a lovely Parsavnath temple. Some of its pieces may be surviving in the pillars or ceilings of the Qutub Minar Complex, where it would have once stood. At the age of twenty-six, when Muni Dada was about to die, he told one of his disciples to stand next to him with a bowl of milk to receive his mani after he died. To others, he instructed that when they carried his dead body on his last journey, they should not place it down anywhere until they reach the final point, else they would not be able to lift it again. However, when the time came, the disciples, lost in their sorrow, forgot Muni Dada's last instruction. When they were passing through the busy market area called

Manek Chowk, people from all around gathered to pay their respects and the disciples obliged them by placing the saint's body at the chowk. When the disciples tried to lift the saint's body, it could not be moved; not even elephants could move it. So, Mani Dada's last rites were performed at the same spot and his samadhi built there. The Dada Bari Temple stands at the same place today, after eight hundred plus years. You can see this story carved on the temple walls. It is difficult to imagine that this place, now surrounded by forests, was once a bustling town with a busy marketplace. Along with the other Jain temples—like the one right in front of the Red Fort in Old Delhi—that managed to survive the most gruesome times during the reign of Aurangzeb, it is a symbol of the resilience of a community that is best known for their adherence to ahimsa or non-violence.

Orchha's Raja Ram Temple has another version of this common story. In the second half of the 16th century, Orchha was ruled by the Rajput king Madhukar Shah, also known as Madhukar Ju. He was a Krishna devotee and had built many temples for his ishta devata. His queen Ganesh Kunwar was an ardent devotee of Sri Ram. She used to participate in the temple rituals of Krishna but her heart was with Sri Ram. Once, Madhukar Ju wanted to go on a pilgrimage to Braj, the land of Krishna. When he asked his queen to join, she refused. In an argument between husband and wife, the king asked the queen that if she was such a big devotee of Sri Ram, why had he not appeared in Orchha yet? Irked, the queen decided to visit Ayodhya and bring her ishta devata Sri Ram along. Before leaving for Ayodhya, she ordered the construction of a Chaturbhuj temple for the deity that she planned to bring back with her. Chaturbhuj refers to the four-armed incarnation of Vishnu, and is a common name in this region. The queen walked to Ayodhya which is a good five hundred kilometers away and stayed there on the banks of the Sarayu like an ascetic, but Sri Ram did not appear before her. It is said that she jumped into the Sarayu River to end her life, and just then, a murti of Sri Ram came into her hands. This was a sign. Ecstatic, she came out of the Sarayu and requested the murti to come with her to Orchha. It is said that Sri Ram agreed to it, on three conditions. One, that he would travel towards Orchha only during Pushya Nakshatra— his birth star. Second, he would be the ruler of Orchha and not her husband Madhukar Ju. The third condition was that he should not be placed down until he reached his rightful place in Orchha, else he would stay where he gets placed. The queen agreed to all his conditions. They traveled only during the said nakshatra, which ensured that it took them months to reach Orchha. Once in Orchha, the queen went to her palace and kept the murti there, to be installed soon in the newly built temple for Sri Ram at an auspicious time. She did not realize her mistake until the murti refused to move out from the queen's palace. So, the temple was built at the same place, and continues to be there till date, in the *ranivasa* or the queen's palace. Sri Ram continues to be the ruler in Orchha even today. He wears the king's attire, and holds a sword in his hand, instead of the bow that he wields in most other places. He is given gun salutes every morning and every evening. You visit this temple as you would visit a king's *durbar*. A couple of generations later, the Orchha kingdom would come into the hands of Bundela Rajput Bir Sing Deo, who completed the Chaturbhuj temple next door and installed a Vishnu murti there. This is the same king who built the most magnificent Keshavdev Temple in Mathura at the birthplace of Krishna, the one that was destroyed by Aurangzeb to raise a mosque over it. Various travelers' chronicles of Mathura talk about the unparalleled grandeur of this temple.

Shrinathji, around whom revolves the temple town of Nathdwara near Udaipur, used to live on a temple atop the Govardhan Hill near Mathura. It is the same hill that Sri Krishna lifted on his little finger to protect the people of

Braj from the anger of Indra. During the invasions of Aurangzeb in Mathura area, many deities were moved from there. When Shrinathji's murti was being brought to Mewar, in the village of Sinhad on the banks of the Banas River, the wheel of the chariot carrying Shrinathji got stuck in the mud and refused to come out. It was taken as a sign that this was the chosen new home of Shrinathji, and a haveli was built for him. The wooden chariot can still be seen in the temple premises. Today, in Nathdwara town, you can see a mini Braj Bhumi thriving. It feels as if the devotees have created the same environment here for Shrinathji, which he used to enjoy in Govardhan.

Natural Foes Turning Friends

This series of stories told me that deities choose to appear at a certain point in time or to live in a particular place, but they also made me wonder why specific places were chosen. Why was this particular place chosen? Why not another place? This reminds me of another series of stories that talk about precisely this—the energy of a space. It has to do with paying attention to pointers, such as when animals which are conventionally natural enemies are seen taking care of each other; this indicates that a sense of love dominates in the land. The place must be holy enough to turn natural foes into friends.

A story goes that Adi Shankaracharya, after traveling around the land of Bharatvarsha, was looking for a place to establish his first institution to perpetuate his Advaita Vedanta philosophy. On the banks of the Tunga River at Sringeri, he saw an unusual sight. A frog was in labor pain, and it was a hot sunny day. A cobra spread its hood over the frog so as to provide shade to the frog and make it comfortable. Now, it is common knowledge that cobras and frogs are natural adversaries. Shankaracharya attributed this benevolent behavior of the cobra to the *satvik* or pious nature of the land, and deemed it appropriate to have his first *matha* set up there, on the banks of the Tunga River. A sculpture on the banks of the river, close to the Sringeri Matha celebrates this story.

On the marble pillar outside the Lal Jain Mandir in Delhi, bang opposite the Red Fort, among the many Jain symbols on it is a sculpture of a cow and a lion drinking milk from the same vessel. In Jain philosophy, this is interpreted as the epitome of non-violence. To me, this also underlined the fact that, in a non-violent world, even natural enemies would live peacefully with each other.

You also hear a reverse version of this story—of places where people lose their natural kindness and become rude or uncaring. The famous story goes that the most obedient son ever, Shravan Kumar, carried his blind parents on his shoulders and took them around different pilgrimage places. Shravan Kumar was shot dead by the arrow of Dashrath, the father of Sri Ram, when he went to fetch water for his parents. His parents cursed Dashrath that he would also die because of separation from his son. Dashrath did indeed die when Sri Ram left for the forest. Shravan Kumar is considered the epitome of an ideal son, who would go to any extent to make his parents happy. People in India often want their sons to be like him.

At some places in India, they say that, once, even Shravan Kumar refused to listen to his parents. He left his parents and walked away, losing his glory as the ideal son. However, as soon as he stepped out of the land that had turned him rude, he realized his mistake, and quickly went back to his parents and took them away from there. Now, I do not know if this is told as a metaphor, or if it is actually mentioned in some version of the story of Shravan Kumar.

Every time I hear such anecdotes, I wonder if the earth does indeed have such an impact on human behavior and animal nature. Is it possible that certain places actually make us better or worse human beings? If yes, that would change the whole connotation associated with traveling to prescribed pilgrimage places. There are local sayings and proverbs that do talk about the nature of some places. Are these just stories told to communicate some values to us, or is there a scientific reason that takes into account the energy fields of the places mentioned?

From my experience, I can say that there are places where you feel elevated and energized, just by being there. For me, Varanasi is one such place where I feel a spring in my feet as soon as I touch it. Mumbai has a restless energy that keeps pushing me, while Goa has this laid-back feel that rarely allows restlessness to creep in. Do the places we live in have an impact on our behavior, or does our collective behavior impact the energy of a place? Is this something that needs to be investigated?

Pandavas' Footprints

I was on a road trip from Shimla to Manali via Kinnaur, Sangla Valley, Lahaul and Spiti, passing through the famous Kunzum Pass that opens only for a small window of time during July–August. Our first stop was Thanedar, not too far from Shimla. On a foggy day, we climbed the Hatu Peak, with the hope that the fog would eventually lift and allow us to take in the beauty of the Himachal landscape. It had other plans though. I saw our first Kathkuni or stone-and-wood temple on its peak, dedicated to Hatu Mata. Surrounded by fog, the temple appeared even more mystical. Inside the temple, there is just a natural rock that is worshipped. The purohit told me that the rock was Draupadi. This is where Draupadi fell and died when the Pandavas were on their way to the Himalayas, after handing over their kingdom to their grandson Parikshit. Over time, she has come to be known as Hatu Mata, and is treated like a deity. This was the Pandava footprint in the Shivalik Range of the Himalayas.

On the same trip, as we reached the mystical Chandratal Lake in the Lahaul region, we heard the story of the Pandavas again. We were told that this was the place where

Indra's chariot descended on earth, to take Yudhishtir, the eldest Pandava, to Swargaloka. It then dawned on me that we had been following the final journey of the Pandavas, though we seemed to have missed the places where the other four Pandavas fell.

During their exiles, both Sri Ram in Ramayana and the Pandavas in Mahabharata traveled across the country. It was almost like an opportunity they seized to travel and acquaint themselves with the vast country. While Ramayana footprints stay on two or three paths connecting Ayodhya to Rameshwaram, Pandava footprints are found across the country. I wonder if there is any part of India that does not carry their footprint, even if it is generally believed that the Pandavas did not really travel southwards.

In a small village called Arvalem in North Goa, six small caves carved out in native laterite stone are known as the Pandava Caves. Five of them, believed to be belonging to the five Pandavas, now have Shivalingas installed in them. Belief is that the brothers stayed here during their *agyat vas* or the last year of their exile and prayed to Shiva. The sixth cave is called Draupadi's Kitchen. Interestingly, it has a kitchen-like platform with depressions carved on it, which look like utensils to hold food. The legend does not end here. The caves are located next to a natural waterfall, creating a pond, which is believed to have been created by Bhim. Bhim Goda is a term used for many water bodies across the country that are attributed to Bhim, as if he alone was responsible for arranging water supply for the family, or perhaps, he was the one who had the power to dig wells and ponds. The most famous of these is the Bhimtal in the Kumaon region of Uttarakhand. It is a huge lake with a Bhimeshwar Mahadev Temple on its banks, indicating that Bhima did indeed live there and installed and worshipped a Shivalinga that is now known by his name.

In the heart of India, close to Bhopal in Madhya Pradesh, you find the famous Bhimbetka Caves where we have pre-historic rock art, an indicator that the land has been inhabited since ages. The hall-like entrance to the caves is believed to be the *baithak* or the living room of Bhim, giving the place its name Bhim Baithak, which later got distorted to Bhimbetka. The Chambal River that flows through the southern slopes of the Vindhyas and covers parts of Madhya Pradesh, Rajasthan, and Uttar Pradesh, is believed to be a cursed river. It is one of the rare rivers that is not worshipped. A legend links it back in time to the Mahabharata. It is believed that it was around this river that the infamous dice game that led to the disrobing of Draupadi took place, and that she cursed the river that her waters would not be drunk and that no one would worship her the way most other rivers are worshipped by the people they nourish. It is up to you to believe or disbelieve this story, but my basic research says that it is true that the river is not worshipped. Ironically, today, it is one of the cleanest rivers in India and boasts of its aquatic biodiversity.

Another place where you find the footprints of the Pandavas is Mahabalipuram, where the earliest stone temples are named after the five brothers, and the most beautiful sculpture on these rockfaces is called Arjuna's penance.

I am yet to read the original Mahabharata, and abridged versions never carry the real locations that the Pandavas traveled to. Even when this is mentioned, it is not easy to map those locations to their current names. However, every pilgrimage site has an intersection with the journeys in these epics; be it in small towns and villages or remote lakes, you always find the footprints of the Pandavas. Technically, we will never be able to figure out if the Pandavas actually traveled to these places or not. Even so, culturally, their travel is so well woven into the warp and weft of this country that one can never be without them, no matter where one stands on this land.

Do these common stories bind us together with some invisible threads? Did the traveling pilgrims carry these stories with them when they traveled? Or did the storytellers at these ancient pilgrimage places tell these stories to the travelers visiting their land? Were the places trying to own a piece of the Mahabharata, and the easiest way was to get the Pandavas to travel to them? Or is it that the descendants of the Kuru dynasty or the residents of Hastinapur traveled and settled all over the land and took their legends along with them?

History Belongs to the Geography

सहस्त्रधारामाराभ्य योजनं पूर्वतो दिशि।
पश्चिमे च तथा देवि योजनं समतोवधि: ।।
दक्षिणोत्तर भागे तु सरयूतमसावधि: ।
ऐतत्क्षेत्रस्य संस्थानं हरेरन्तर्ग्रहं स्मृतम।।

—Skand Puran, Ayodhya Mahatmay

Beginning from Sahastradhara, one yojana to the east, one yojana to the west till Sama, Sarayu to the South and Tamasa to the North, this is the inner sanctum where Hari lives.

The text goes on the describe the fish-like shape of the city of Ayodhya.

Traveling across India is akin to getting a first-hand taste of the history of the lands visited. Initially, when I traveled to places in South India or North East India, or to some remote corner of the country rarely visited by outsiders, with each new discovery, I wondered why no one had taught me about the various dynasties of these regions, all of whom have left behind amazing legacies. Some of these dynastic names like the Ahoms of Assam were completely alien to me. I questioned those who wrote our textbooks for their choice of restricting our textbooks to a small region, and to an even smaller period of time. I wondered if my school history teacher was even aware of these wonderful dynasties.

As I traveled more and more, and discovered more and more amazing kings, commoners, innovators, and spiritual gurus, I came to understand that it is not easy to fit them all into one set of books. India is too old, too layered, too diverse, and hence too complicated to fit into any history textbook. I realized this has to be a lifelong exploration for those who choose to explore. All these marvels from the pages of our history cannot be served to you on a platter in a few pages. You must go out and seek, you must make the effort to find out. Yes, the history of India demands that you get up, step out of your comfort zone, romance a little with the pieces of heritage you see scattered around, and then, it starts revealing itself to you. It asks you to come with an open mind, not limited by what you already know. Insight into history is something that you find on the way, that you stumble upon as you wander around with a longing in your heart.

The Ramayana and the Mahabharata, our two epics, comfort us in an amazingly unique way when we travel to new regions in India. These two stories are ubiquitously familiar to everyone, to even those who are not followers of Sanatana Dharma. Most people identify with one or another of the characters in these epics, and vice versa, use their names to identify people who sport traits associated with these characters. When someone is called Shakuni mama, you instantly understand the person to be scheming and to be driven by an emotion of revenge. When someone is called Hanuman, you know that the person is dependable and capable of lifting mountains if need be. Vibhishana is often referred to as someone who can be solely responsible for destroying his own kingdom. You do not have to explain these characters or related episodes from the two epics, they are a part of our psyche, our languages.

The credit for keeping the two epics alive must go to the different types of performing art forms across the length and breadth of India, and especially to our folk artists, who still follow oral traditions in a sense. If the Ramayana is performed as Ram Leela in North India, Kathakali dancers of Kerala recreate the stories of Mahabharata in their nightlong performances, and Manipuri dancers recreate the Ras Leela of Krishna, just like dancers in Braj Bhumi in Uttar Pradesh and on the western tip of India in Dwarka.

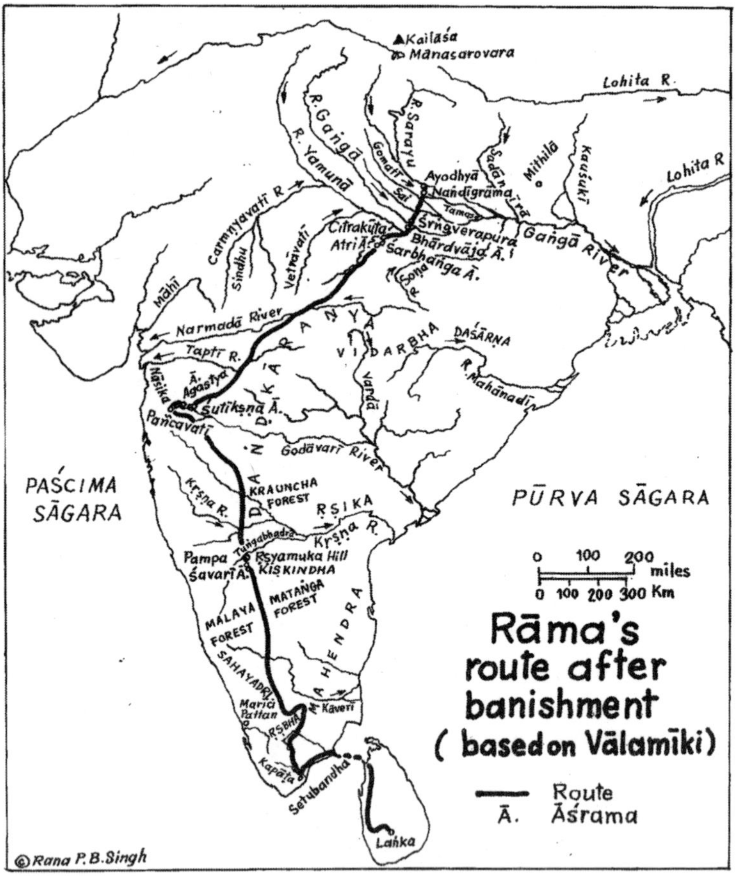

Ramayana Map. Reproduced with courtesy and permission from Singh, Rana P.B. 1991. © Singh, Rana P.B.

The geography of the Ramayana runs north-south across the Indian subcontinent. The story begins from Ayodhya where Raja Dashrath wished for a son. The story goes on to Janakpur in Nepal for the wedding of Sri Ram and Sita Devi. The exile path of Sri Ram runs south, through various forests. It pauses at various ashrams like Bharadwaj Ashram in Prayag and at Panchvati near present-day Nashik where Sita ji is abducted by Ravana. Kishkindha, that would be present day Hampi in Karnataka, is where it stops for a while before moving further south to Sri Lanka. It covers the India of its times, north to south, not really touching the Himalayas.

The Mahabharata, on the other hand, runs horizontally—east to west. Its focal point is Hastinapur and Indraprastha, which would be Western Uttar Pradesh and Delhi respectively, of our times. However, its stories and sub-plots take you from Gandhar that would be Kandahar in Afghanistan today, and goes up to Manipur on the eastern margins of India. The Pandavas, during their exile, lived in various Himalayan ranges. Arjuna did travel southwards up to about Dwarka in Gujarat, to Krishna's kingdom. Of course, the Mahabharata war took place in Kurukshetra, not too far from their own kingdom. Kurukshetra is located on the Uttarpath, the grand ancestor of the famous Grand Trunk Road or the national highway that runs from Amritsar to Kolkata now. As I said, no matter where you travel in India, you will find some reference to it being visited by the Pandavas during their exile. Almost anything ancient—like a cave, a pond, or a painting in the country—is more often than not wrapped in some story concerning the Pandavas' visit.

The geographies of the two epics meet at Kashi. We find that the daughters of Kashi were married into the protagonist families of the epics. Sumitra, the mother of Lakshman and Shatrughan in Ramayana was a princess of

Kashi. Ambika and Ambalika, the mothers of Dhritrashtra and Pandu respectively, were also princesses of Kashi. Kashi or present-day Varanasi happens to be a place where, roughly, Uttarpath and Dakshinpath—Bharat's two major ancient trade routes, running east-west and north-south respectively, met.

What I found interesting during my travels is that the epics continue to thrive, owing to the fact that they are still alive and throbbing in the key places associated with them. This vitality does not stem from just a simple association of the place with the epic or its characters, it is also about how the epics and their characters are still being referred to, worshipped, or associated with. It is also about how the principal deities of worship differ from place to place, in tandem with the epics' stories. This choice, as I discovered, is not coincidental, it is closely related to the lived past of these epics.

Ram Ram

In Ayodhya, Sri Ram is revered in two forms—as Ram Lalla and as Raja Ram. Ram Lalla is how he is fondly called at his birthplace, which is exactly how infants continue to be addressed even today in this region. He is also addressed as Raja Ram, because, as a king, he ruled from Ayodhya. This was his capital, from where he, as well as his illustrious ancestors had ruled for eons. Interestingly, in Ayodhya, his name is always taken with Sita. There is a tradition of writing Sita Ram on bilva leaves before offering it to Shivalinga in the Shiva temples of Ayodhya. I visited many temples across the city, and it was always "Sita Ram" and never "Sri Ram" or "Ram Ram." Even in their greetings, most of the time, people in this region say "Sita Ram," while in many other places across India, "Ram Ram" and "Jai Shri Ram" are more popular.

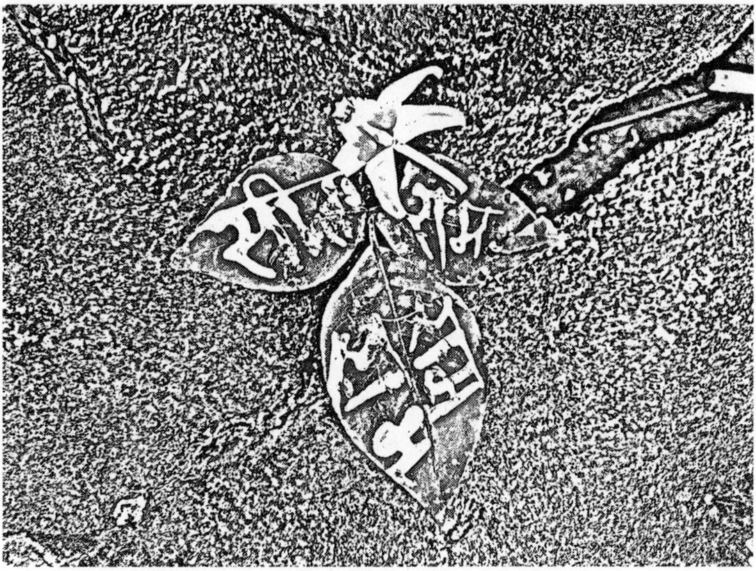

Bilva leaves with Ram Ram written on it

The only other place where Sri Ram is called Raja Ram is Orchha. Remember the story of how he came to be the king of Orchha, which we saw in an earlier chapter? Even today, when you speak to an average person in Awadh, you realize that, though he knows that Sri Ram was away for fourteen years and traveled to Lanka during this time, but for him, this is but a fleeting part of Ram's life. What is more important for him is that Sri Ram was born here and that he ruled from here. Even when he was away, his *khadaun*—his wooden slippers—ruled on his behalf. You can visit Nandigram, the place where his younger brother Bharat lived outside the city limits of Ayodhya in a simple *kuti* or hut while Sri Ram was away on exile, refusing to stay in the luxury of the city while his elder brother was away.

Hada-Hadai is a unique festival celebrated in Ayodhya eleven days after Deepawali. It is said that after the return of Sri Ram along with his new friends from Kishkindha and

Lanka, the people of Ayodhya were curious to know about the war in Lanka. They were eager to know how the famous golden Lanka of Ravan was first burnt by Hanuman and then won by the *vanar sena*, the army of the monkeys. They were also curious what the famous Lanka looked like. It is believed that Hanuman and the other monkeys re-enacted Lanka *dahan* for the people of Ayodhya, to show them how Lanka was conquered. This tradition continues to date, with Lanka dahan or the burning of Lanka being reenacted for the people of Ayodhya during the Hada-Hadai festival, that happens here during the same time as the annual Kartik Mela. This is something that happens only in Ayodhya and nowhere else, for who else would have had the privilege of hearing a first-hand narration of the war from those who actually fought it? Most of us would get to read or hear only the later versions handed down to us.

In Mithila, the home of Sita, Sri Ram is always seen as *var roop* or son-in-law. Even in Mithila's painting and other art forms, the favorite scenes are those of Ram-Janaki wedding. Goswami Tulsidas devotes a large part of his Ramcharitmanas to describe the city of Janakpur, the first meeting of Ram and Sita in a garden, the breaking of Shiva's bow Pinaki, the anger of Parshuram, and the elaborate wedding rituals. As is the tradition, the women of Mithila tease Sri Ram, the son-in-law. I remember my guide in Ayodhya telling me that the women of Mithila were blessed in many ways because not only did one of them get to be the wife of Sri Ram, it also gave them all the right to tease him and say naughty things to him. No one else can do that to the righteous king Sri Ram. On another occasion, a senior Uttar Pradesh official shared with me an anecdote regarding inviting the Mahant of Janaki Mandir in Janakpur for a program in Ayodhya. By some oversight, they forgot to pay the expenses for his travel. Many days later, when they realized this oversight and wanted to pay him for his travel expenses, he had said, *"Mein beti ke ghar se kaise le sakta hun?"* meaning "How can I take anything from a daughter's home?" The mahant was referring to a tradition wherein parents do not take anything from a family they have given their daughter in marriage to. The daughter here, mind you, is Sita, the one who married Sri Ram of Ayodhya in Tretayuga, an age we do not even have an agreement on how far back it goes in history. This makes for a fragile yet enduring thread of living culture that is rooted in a distant but shared past.

When you move along the route that Sri Ram took during his exile, you see him as a bow-weilding Ram—someone who is dressed like a sadhu but carries a bow. Here, he is a wanderer, a forest dweller. In much of South India and its temples, images, paintings and murtis, you find depictions of Sri Ram as *Kodand* Ram, that is, Sri Ram with a bow in his hands. This is how South Indians saw him—holding a bow in his hand, in search of his wife—and this is how they remember him. It does not matter that, over time, they learnt the rest of his story. The part of the Ramayana story that belongs to them is when Sri Ram was walking through forests, carrying a bow.

Is it just a random phenomenon that different regions look at different aspects of the same deity and his story? Are they not carrying forward a tradition that has its roots in the times these epic stories actually took place? Why else should aspects worshipped of the same deity vary from region to region, and perfectly concord with his journey through that geography?

Krishna's Wanderings

Let us now look at the places associated with Krishna. Krishna was born in Mathura. A temple dedicated to his birthplace, in this city on the banks of the Yamuna River, celebrates his birth. It is duly recreated as a prison since he took birth in a prison where his parents Vasudev and Devaki had been kept confined by his uncle Kamsa. The temple has seen many a turmoil as it was the prime target of Mughal kings who ruled from the close-by cities of Agra and Delhi. However, it has always managed to make a comeback at the same place, thanks to the immense faith that Sri Krishna's devotees have in him.

From Mathura, across the Yamuna river, in the village of Gokul, where Sri Krishna was brought to as a newborn and exchanged with the daughter of Nanda and Yashoda, he continues to be celebrated as an infant. His murtis in the temples of the village of Gokul are mostly as *bal* Krishna or baby Krishna, affectionately called "Laddu Gopal." I was told that during the Holi festival, when Lath Maar Holi is played in Braj with Lath or big bamboo sticks, women beat men with wet sticks to their heart's content. In Gokul, it is played as Chhari Maar Holi. *Chhari* is a smaller, milder, and softer version of the *lath*, which is a big and hard bamboo stick. After all, Krishna was a baby in Gokul, so the stick should not hurt him in any way. Chhari Maar Holi is played only in the village of Gokul where Krishna lived as an infant.

Braj Bhumi, that is spread over an area with a circumference of eighty-four Kos—which is roughly three hundred kilometers—around the cities of Mathura and Vrindavan, is full of stories of Krishna, Radha and their *leela*. Little ahead of Gokul is the village of Baldeva, an area named after Krishna's elder brother Balram. In this village, it is his temple that takes center stage. Balram and his wife Revati are the presiding deities of this temple that hosts the grand finale of the Holi festival in Braj, called Dauji Ka Huranga.

In Barsana, the village of Radha, her temple—where she is in the form of Kishori ji or the eternal youthful teenager—sits on the high Brahma Hill. She is the reigning queen of the region, being the only one capable of controlling and influencing Krishna. The region around Barsana is full of love stories of Radha and Krishna. For instance, a pond called Peeli Pokhar is so called because, it is believed that it is here that Sri Radha washed her turmeric makeup after meeting Krishna. Braj region used to be full of several different forests called *vanas*, each of which narrate stories of the revelries of Radha and Krishna. Meanwhile, Govardhan Parvat, the hill that was held up by Krishna on his little finger, is surrounded by temples showing him holding up the hill.

Vrindavan, which used to be a van or a forest, and is one of the many forests that form Braj Bhumi, is now full of temples dedicated to Radha Krishna. Vrindavan primarily came up after Chaitanya Mahaprabhu rediscovered this region early in the 16th century. This is a place that celebrates the love of Radha and Krishna for each other, the love of the Gopis of Braj for Krishna, the motherly love of Yashoda for Krishna, and the love of *Brajwasis* for their favorite son of the soil. Devotees who come here see him from different *bhavas* or emotions.

I met Anurag Sakhi, a sadhu, at the temple of Radha Rani in Barsana. He explained to me the different emotions with which devotees of Krishna relate to him. Some see him with *vatsalya bhava* or motherly emotion—they see Krishna as a child; to them, he is always bal Krishna or baby Krishna who must be taken care of, just like how a mother takes care of and pampers her young ones. Radha saw Krishna through *madhurya bhava*—the sweet emotion that looks at the beloved as the source of all happiness. This is an inherited emotion with which many devotees approach Krishna. They see in him the source of all their happiness. Their goal in life is to reach him. When Krishna plays his flute, he is evoking the madhurya bhava in his devotees. It is not unusual to see his devotees, both men and women, dressed as Gopis and dancing with Krishna, and for Krishna. Young boys and girls of Braj saw Krishna with *sakha bhava* or as friends, as did Sudama and Arjuna. You too can choose to be friends with him, play with him, and fool around with him. Some devotees choose *dasya bhava*, they see him as their master who they wish to serve. We see this emotion prominently in how Hanuman relates to Sri Ram; nevertheless, this bhava can be adopted for any deity you chose as your ishta devata. *Shanta bhava* is seen in Dwarka, the emotion involved when the subjects relate to their king, knowing that he will take care of them. It is an emotion of being carefree, which comes from knowing that someone up there is taking care of you, just like how children feel protected when their parents are around.

In Dwarka, the golden city that Krishna built on the coast of Saurashtra, he rules. He is mostly called Dwarkadhish—the lord of Dwarka. He is not called a king, for he was never coronated as the king; that position stayed with his father, and his elder brother was the heir apparent to the throne. So, Krishna is called Dwarkadhish, the one to whom Dwarka bows to. Dwarka belongs to him irrespective of the sitting ruler. This always impresses me with the thought that you do not have to hold a position to rule the hearts of people. In Gujarat, Krishna is fondly called Ranchorrai, which literally means 'The one who ran away from the battlefield'. This name comes from the fact that he ran away from a battlefield in Mathura, tired of fighting endless battles with his uncle Jarasandh, and decided to settle in Dwarka. I always find it strange that such a name is actually used and used as fondly as his other names. You rarely find this name used anywhere outside of Saurashtra. Nonetheless, Dwarka was his kingdom, the one he himself built from scratch. This is the city where he lived with his family—his eight wives, his parents Devaki and Vasudev, his brother Balram and sister-in-law Revati, his sixteen thousand other wives who came from Kamrup, and his many sons. His Guru Durvasa lived not too far from the city. In Dwarka, Sri Krishna is a complete family man, nothing like his carefree naughty self in Braj. Here, Rukmini is his prime consort. You always see Rukmini next to him. Ironically, she is absent in the main Dwarkadhish temple, but then, she has her own temple on the outskirts of the city. Radha takes a backseat in the minds of people here, and hence also in the temples of Dwarka, similar to how you hardly find Rukmini in the temples of Braj. One of the biggest festivals in Dwarka is Rukmini Vivah that celebrates the wedding of Krishna and Rukmini. Rukmini was the princess of Vidarbha, and she asked Krishna to abduct her from her planned wedding with Shishupal of the Chedi kingdom. He complied and abducted her. On their way to Dwarka, their first stop was Madhavpura, a little before Dwarka, where they got married, and the wedding is still celebrated as a big event here, every year. You can even come across their wedding invitations on the streets of Dwarka and Madhavpura, days before the Rukmini Vivah festival.

Speaking of the Chedi Kingdom, which would be present-day Odisha region, it takes us to Puri where Krishna lives with his siblings Balbhadra and Subhadra. Every temple here belongs to the three siblings. The popular temple activities of this region revolve around the siblings; for instance, its world famous Rath Jatra is all about the siblings' annual visit to their aunt's place. Every time I hear the story of Puri's Rath Jatra, I am reminded of my own annual school holidays and my visit to my grandparents' and other relatives' homes. Here, Radha, Rukmini, Gopis—all of them take a back seat. This place is all about celebrating the sibling relationship and their daily and annual routines; no wonder, food takes center stage here.

We know Porbandar as the birthplace of Mahatma Gandhi, but it is also the town of Krishna's childhood friend—Sudama. You see him in sakha roop or as a friend here. At Sandipani Ashram near Ujjain, Krishna is a student just like any other student.

When you join the dots, you understand that the people of these ancient cities of India are celebrating what their distant ancestors must have actually seen during their lifetimes. People in Dwarka are not bothered about what

Krishna did before he came to Dwarka, and people of Braj are not concerned with what he did after he left Braj. He continues to live in their memories and celebrations just the way he lived in Braj and Dwarka, respectively. I find this continuity to be an incredible thread of a living civilization. These are traditions that continue to thrive just as they did thousands of years ago; we do not even know how many thousands. No matter how many invasions, interruptions or disasters—natural or man-made—these lands saw, some strands managed to survive, almost like a recessive gene that manages to hide itself until it feels safe enough to show up again. In that sense, history truly belongs to the geography where it took place.

Holi is celebrated across India in diverse forms, but the epicenter of Holi remains the Braj region. It is here that it lasts for about forty days, culminating on the day of Falgun Purnima—the day the whole of India celebrates Holi. I always thought this was about celebrating the playful Holi of Radha and Krishna, including the famous Lathmar Holi played between their respective villages—Nand Gaon and Barsana—which continues to loom large in the minds of the people here. But little did I realize that I was missing the main ritual of the Holi festival—Holika Dahan. Well, we all assume that this must have taken place at some fictional point in space and time. At least, I thought so, until I studied all the different types of Holi played in Braj. In a small village called Falen here, there is a Prahalad Mandir and a Prahalad Kund. This is believed to be the place where Holika, sister of the asura Hiranayakashyap, entered the fire with her nephew Prahalad. If you have written an essay on Holi during your school days, you would remember the story that Holika had a boon that fire could not kill her. However, this time, when she entered the fire with an intention to kill Prahalad, she perished, and Prahalad, a devout Vishnu *bhakta,* survived. This is the origin of the festival of Holi. In Falen village, every year, on the day of Holi, a *panda* enters the giant fire that is lit up next to the village pond and comes out unharmed! The purohit performing this ritual, of course, follows elaborate rituals of fasting, taking a dip in the holy pond and staying satvik. I am not aware of any other place that follows something similar on Holi. You could say there is no place that celebrates Holi like Braj Bhumi does. Is it because this festival is rooted here in this land, and so this is where it continues to be closest to the hearts of people? Is this why it attracts travelers from around the world for the festivities?

Gokul village of Braj on the south bank of the Yamuna resonates with the same emotions as that of the distant village of Thiruvalla in Kerala, not too far from the extremely popular Sabrimala Temple. On the outskirts of this village lies the temple of Alamthuruthy Bhagwathy, who is believed to be Yogmaya, the incarnation of the girl who was exchanged with Krishna at birth, the one who flew away from the hands of Kamsa after declaring that his slayer had already taken birth. Some of her popular temples include the one at Mehrauli in Delhi and another on the Vindhyachal Parvat near Varanasi where she is worshipped as Vindhyavasini. Now, at this Kerala temple, she is treated as an infant or a newborn girl. So, all the temple rituals here take a detour from the standard practices of this region, such as elephant processions and bursting of crackers, as the deity here is a baby, and these things might scare her. During her annual yatra, when she visits Mahavishnu at Sri Vallabha Temple in the village, she is carried carefully in a palanquin. Being a child, she is allowed to visit the deity in his garbhagriha; again, this is something that goes against usual norms, where the visiting deity usually stays outside the garbhagriha. It amazes me how the rituals for deities who are worshipped as infants are so similar, even though their temples are far apart, and that these rituals are so sensitive to their stage in life.

Frozen Moments from the Past

Devi Bhagwat Puran has an elaborate account of the

Swayamvara of Shashikala, the daughter of Subahu—the Kashi Naresh or King of Kashi. Subahu organized an *iccha swayamvara* for his daughter, wherein it is the woman's prerogative to simply choose the groom she wants. Shashikala wanted to marry Sudarshan, the exiled prince of Ayodhya who had grown up with his widowed mother Manorama in Prayag, at the ashram of Bharadwaj Muni. It is the same Bharadwaj Ashram that Sri Ram had visited on his way to, and also on his way back from Sri Lanka. Sudarshan is a Devi bhakta, a devotee of Shakti. Both Sudarshan and Shashikala, in their dreams, get directions from the Devi to marry each other. Shashikala conveys the same to her parents. However, her father has already invited kings and princes from around the country for her swayamvara. They, like most parents, are under social pressure to let a fair swayamvara happen as planned. Coronated kings who have traveled from across the country to marry Shashikala do not allow Sudarshan to take part in the swayamvara, as devoid of any kingdom to rule, he is not on par with them. Eventually, the couple convince the parents that their union is the will of the Devi, and they get married before the swayamvara. As expected, all the kings gathered in Kashi for the event, including the stepbrother of Sudarshan and his maternal uncle, who had been instrumental in throwing him out of Ayodhya, are ready to kill Sudarshan and claim Shashikala. Shashikala was considered an incarnation of Lakshmi, the goddess of prosperity, and every prince present wanted to have her by his side. A battle follows and the Devi appears on the battleground as Durga and kills all the enemies. Subahu, the Kashi Naresh, is awestruck at the sight of Devi. All he can do is sing a Devi stuti, or verses in praise of the Devi, while acknowledging the fact that it was because of his son-in-law's devotion that he got to witness the Devi in her manifestation as Durga riding the lion. He then requests the Devi to stay back in Kashi, and she obliges. The famous red and gold Durga temple next to Durga Kund in Kashi is believed to be the very same temple that Subahu had built for the Devi. It is one of the nine Nav Durga temples in the city of Shiva. Incidentally, I visited this temple while reading this episode of Devi Bhagwat. To me, this is a frozen moment from history—when Durga descended on earth to protect dharma by protecting her bhaktas who are ardent followers of dharma.

Kanchipuram is a unique temple town. At the heart of it is the Kanchi Kamakshi Temple. Surrounding this temple are two distinct Kanchi sub-cities—Shiva Kanchi and Vishnu Kanchi. Within each of these sub-cities, while the temples dedicated to its presiding deity dominate, temples dedicated to the other deities are not missing. So, Vishnu Kanchi does have temples like Vyaseshawara or Punyakotishwara dedicated to Shiva, and Shiva Kanchi has temples like Pandavadoota Perumal Temple. Now, this Pandavadoota Temple intrigued me when I stood in front of this lovely stone temple from a distant past. The priest explained that this temple celebrates the moment when Krishna visited Kauravas at Hastinapur as the *doota* or messenger of the Pandavas. You will remember this from the Mahabharata as a visit that happened just before the war, a final effort on the part of Krishna to avoid the war. Now, the Mahabharata war happened at Kurukshetra. Hastinapur was somewhere in present-day western Uttar Pradesh and Krishna's kingdom was in coastal Gujarat in Dwarka. Thousands of kilometers south-east of these places, in Tamil Nadu, a temple was built to commemorate that visit of Krishna to Hastinapur as the messenger of the Pandavas. This is another frozen-in-time temple that also tells you that the Mahabharata was well-known and well-understood in this part of the country. Why someone would choose this one moment to freeze in stone is something I am yet to discover. I can only guess that it was someone who was inspired by that final attempt by Krishna to solve the problem peacefully. Perhaps, that incident from the ancient past helped solve a dispute peacefully sometime in the more recent past of Kanchipuram. Then of course, there is the story of the Kopeshwar Mahadev Temple, where the moment of Sati's immolation is frozen in time, as we saw earlier on in this book.

Stories from India's past are scattered across her geography, the very same geography that was an integral part of these stories. Through the lived experience, you can see a perfect mapping of these historic stories on the geography where they took place. This pattern is not very apparent till you step out and travel to these places and experience the rootedness of these stories in the places associated with them. Until you visit them, these are mythical places and mythical stories belonging to another space and time. Once you step foot on these lands, you realize that these stories are alive in much the same way we are living and breathing descendants of our ancestors of the same space and time these stories were set in. You see glimpses of long-standing traditions in every aspect of life there—be it the way people dress, the way they speak, or the way they relate to the presiding deity of the land. If my history books gave me disconnected and disoriented bites to chew, my travels joined the pieces together as a single narrative, like a beautiful fabric fluttering in the sky, with a million stories lending their colors to it.

When Deities Too Travel

घुष्यते यस्य नगरे रंगयात्रा दिने दिने ।
तमहम्सिरसा वन्दे राजानं कुलशेखरम् ॥

—Mukundamala

I bow down to King Kulashekhara, in whose kingdom the yatra of Sri Ranga is celebrated every day.

Deities, in our culture, are not just divine but are living beings too, just like us. They may be carved in stone, wood, metal, or a combination of metals, but once their eyes are opened by the *sthapati* and the pran pratishtha is done, they become living beings. They follow daily routines of waking up early in the morning, getting ready for the day, eating three or more meals a day, listening to devotees who have come to meet them, and playing with their fellow deities in the temple before retiring for the day. Every temple has its own, unique daily routine that is usually as per the *agama* and *nigama shastras* the temple follows. Deviations are often associated with the individual stories of the temples. Some deities have entertainment as a part of their routine. For instance, Shiva and Parvati play a game of *chaupar* at night at the Omkareshwar Temple on the banks of the Narmada. Not all deities get up early in the morning. A case in point is the Banke Bihari Temple in Vrindavan, where there are no early morning rituals, as Krishna here likes to get up late.

Temples are the homes of deities, where they live with their families and friends. At Dwarka temples, you see the whole extended family of Krishna along with his *kul guru* and his *kul devi*. At Ayodhya, you see Ram durbar with all the four brothers, three mothers, and Hanuman—along with many others of Ram's court. At most Shiva temples, you also see temples dedicated to Parvati and their two sons, Ganesh and Kartik. They are called *parivar devatas* or family deities. Deities regularly step out of their *garbhagrihas* or sanctums to take a walk, which also serves the purpose of giving *darshan* to devotees. At places, it is seen as a kind of inspection routine to see that all is well in their jurisdiction. Most deities have a weekly routine of going around the neighborhood. For example, most Devi temples have a *palki* procession on Fridays. Shiva temples follow this routine on Mondays. Ekadashi or the 11th day of the lunar fortnight is observed spiritedly in almost all Vishnu temples. There are annual festivals too when the deities go for a larger *nagar parikrama*. In ancient temples that still have living temple tanks, deities go for a *nauka vihar* or boat ride as a leisure activity, and to give darshan to their devotees as well. In temples of Kerala that are surrounded by backwaters, deities go for a boat ride on the backwaters.

Deities lead a life just like their devotees do, staying at home most of the time, and taking occasional breaks. It also brings in a kind of balance between the deity-devotee relationship. While devotees visit the deity most of the time, at defined times, deities too step out to meet the devotees.

Deities travel just like we do, and for pretty much the same reasons. Just like us, deities visit their families who live away from them. They periodically travel as part of their routine to breathe in some fresh air. They also change their residence once in a while. Sometimes, they move to please their devotees in another place; sometimes, they give in to the demands of an adamant but loving devotee. Some of them even divide their time between multiple temples.

There have been unfortunate times, though, when deities have been forced to move due to circumstances like invasions and attacks on temples. Some of these deities had to stay in hiding for a long period of time, hidden inside in a well, an underground bunker, or a small hut, before their homes were restored to them. Many of them are still waiting for their rightful homes. This is a distressing aspect about temple deities that I observed as I traveled across temples, listening to their stories.

Sri Jagannath of Puri famously visits his *mausi* or maternal aunt at her home called Gundicha Temple—which is some three kilometers away from his own temple—for nine days. His visit has a fixed date, Ashadh Shukla Dwitiya or the second day of the bright fortnight of the month of Ashadh, which usually falls in July. Every year, when I hear about this grand Puri yatra, I am struck by how it sounds like our annual summer vacation visits to relatives' homes. This annual *rath* yatra is the biggest festival of the Jagannath Puri Temple. The Gundicha Temple is duly prepared for this annual visit of Jagannath, just like how our grandmothers would keep their laddus ready for our visits. On the way, Jagannath, along with his siblings, stops at a small temple dedicated to Mausi Ma, where they are served their favorite food. To me, our summer vacation visits to our relatives' homes are nothing but a continuation of this tradition.

At Kolhapur, Mahalakshmi visits her younger sister Triambuli Devi at her temple, which is a few kilometers away, on Lalita Panchami or the fifth day of the Sharad Navaratri. On the way, she is offered prayers by the royal family of Kolhapur. The Triambuli Devi Temple has a dedicated platform where Mahalakshmi sits when she is visiting. It is not used for any other purpose. I saw a similar platform at the Sanjeevi Raya Anjaneya Temple in Aiyangarkulam village in Tamil Nadu, where Varadaraja Perumal, the presiding deity of the famous Vishnu Kanchi, visits once a year on Chaitra Purnima. He takes a bath in the Nata Bhavi stepwell close by and stays on the platform for some time before heading back home. This is like an annual outing to take a swim and visit his devotee Hanuman.

Some stories tell you the reason why these deities visit these temples. In the case of Mahalakshmi, Triambuli Devi was the daughter of the ruler of this region who helped Mahalakshmi kill the Kolhasur asura. Devi forgot about her after the war ended, which annoyed Triambuli Devi. To pacify her, Devi promised that she would visit her every year on the tithi of Lalita Panchami, and she keeps her promise.

Deities living high up in the Himalayas come downhill to spend winters. For instance, Badrinath ji comes down to Joshimath and stays at the Narasimha Temple here, until the doors of his hill abode open again in summer. At the Kinner Kailash range of the Himalayas in Himachal Pradesh, people here believe it to be the winter home of Shiva that he comes to, when Kailash Parvat— Mount Kailash—the home of Shiva—gets too cold to live. So, it seems, deities too have seasonal homes, like the uber-rich.

There are deities who divide their time between different locations, just like how people with businesses in multiple places, or politicians with large territories to look after, divide their time. Ram as Raja Ram divides his time between Ayodhya and Orchha. It is believed that he spends his days in Ayodhya and comes back to Orchha every evening. Likewise, Sharada Amma divides her time between her temple at Mookambika in Karnataka and Chotanikkara at Kochi. At the later temple, she spends her mornings, and for her morning *shringar here,* Devi is always in a white sari. Does this remind you of any temple where deities do not live permanently, but visit regularly?

Apart from their regular travel schedules, deities sometimes move to altogether new places when their devotees need them, and they are pleased enough to oblige them. Raghunathji temple in Kullu, the venue of the famous Kullu Dussehra, has an interesting story about how Raghunathji came to Kullu. Raja Jagat Singh used to rule Kullu during the mid-17th century. A brahmin named Durga Dutt in his kingdom was tortured for the alleged possession of a treasure. Unable to disprove it, the brahmin committed suicide along with his family, but not before cursing the king. The curse materialized immediately, and the king could not eat anything. He would see insects and blood in his food, just as the brahmin had pronounced in his curse. Troubled, he contacted another mahatma for its resolution, who in turn read it as a result of *brahmana hatya* or killing of a brahmin, one of the most heinous of crimes a person can commit. As a remedy, he suggested the bringing of a murti of Raghunathji from Ayodhya, installing it in Kullu and coronating the murti of Raghunathji as the king of Kullu.

Visiting Ayodhya from Kullu was not easy in those days, so a disciple of the mahatma named Damodar was entrusted with this task. He spent many days traveling to Ayodhya and managed to get the golden murtis of Sri Ram and Sita Devi. The same were installed in the royal palace on the day of Dussehra in 1660 CE, and since then, Kullu Dussehra is celebrated in a grand way. In fact, kings of Kullu now act as the *chharibardar* or vice-regents of Raghunathji. The eldest son of the family inherits this position by default. In Kullu, it is believed that all the 365 deities of the Kullu Hills attend the Kullu Dussehra. They come in their palanquins, and a *natti* dance is duly performed to welcome them.

Across North India, Ravana is symbolically killed by Ram on the tenth day of Dussehra by firing an arrow on to large effigies of Ravana, Kumbhakaran and Meghnad. In Kullu, Raghunathji travels to the banks of the Beas River, where a symbolic Lanka has been created to be destroyed. People in Kullu also believe that these murtis were made by

Sri Ram himself for the Ashwamedha Yagna. To me, this is an example of deities traveling to be with their devotees, much like parents leaving their own homes to move in with their children, to support them.

Udupi is a small coastal town in Karnataka. Life here revolves around the Krishna Temple at Sri Krishna Mutt, though you may know this town better for the famous South Indian restaurants it lends its name to—Udupi restaurants. Dosa here remains as famous as ever. About twenty years ago, when I first visited it, I had to wear the *mundu* to enter the temple, but lately they have let go of that requirement; this time, I could visit in my chudidhar-kurta. A case of how temples keep changing with the times. The story of Sri Krishna here is as fascinating as that of Raghunathji in Kullu, the difference being that, here, Sri Krishna himself chose the place and the devotees to live with. It is believed that this murti was in Dwarka, and Rukmini, the chief queen of Sri Krishna used to worship it. She used to apply sandalwood paste called Gopi chandan on it every day, and over time, the murti became covered by a thick layer of Gopi chandan. After a while, it started looking like a solid ball of sandalwood. When Dwarka was engulfed by the sea and became submerged, this ball with Sri Krishna murti too went under the sea. It floated and eventually reached the Malpe Beach near Udupi. Now, there are various versions of how the murti traveled from Dwarka to Malpe Beach. One version says that a ship carried it from Dwarka to Malpe, while another says that a ship caught in a storm could be anchored at Malpe only after it touched this ball containing the murti. Some say that the 13th century saint Madhawacharya helped the ship out of the storm with his powers and asked for this ball in return. You can choose the version you want to believe in. The long story short is that the Krishna murti reached Malpe beach from Dwarka, where it was received by Sri Madhawacharya. He left it in a pond to be washed, and when the murti emerged sans all the sandalwood paste, it was duly installed, and a temple was built for the murti.

As is customary, the murti was originally facing east, the direction of the rising sun. Then came a twist. Once, a devotee named Kanakdasa was not allowed to enter the temple. Krishna did not like his devotee being denied his darshan. It is said that the murti thereupon turned around and gave darshan to Kanakdasa through a window on the temple's posterior wall. Since then, the murti stands facing the west, against norms. Such is the relationship between a deity and a devotee—the deity can not only choose the devotees to live with, but also change established norms, if need be, to please a devotee or to be fair to his devotees.

Kamru Fort is a small wooden hill fort in the remote Sangla Valley of Himachal Pradesh on the banks of the Baspa River. It was the seat of power of the royal family before the capital was moved a little downhill to Rampur Bushahr. Here, a small temple dedicated to Kamakhya Devi continues to be a practicing temple, even though the hill fort has completely fallen out of use. You are required to wear the green *kinnauri* cap on your head and a silk belt called *gachi* before entering the temple. The beautiful murti of Kamakhya was brought here by a king from the Kamrup region or present-day Assam, where Kamakhya is the presiding deity. This incident illustrates the tradition of bringing your ishta devata from his kshetra, his primary home, to your place. This practice is followed by many royal families, or perhaps it is only their records that have managed to survive. By way of the same tradition, the Maharaja of Patiala brought a Kali murti for the famous Kali temple of Patiala from Kolkata, where she is the reigning deity. In such instances, the deities have not really left their own seats, but have allowed their followers to carry an image of them so as to experience the deities' constant presence in their own kingdoms or homes. This is akin to picking up small photographs or murtis sold outside famous temples, for placing in our own personal temples. When kings did this, they also built big temples for these deities.

So far, we saw the travels that deities undertake either of their own will or by the will and devotion of their devotees. This was not the case always. Sometimes they were moved as a symbol of war booty. When the victor belonged to the same faith, they continued to get respect from the new king, though perhaps in a different place, and in a different manner. If the victor were a devotee of the same deity as the loser, the deity would travel back with the victor and get a new home in the victor's capital. For example, when Krishnadevaraya of Vijayanagar won a war against the Gajapati kings of Kalinga, he brought the Bal Krishna murti from there with him and reverentially built a temple for it—the famous Vithala Temple Complex in his capital at Hampi. That it was subsequently lost during an attack on the Vijayanagar kingdom is another story.

Most successive kings contributed to pleasing the deities by giving grants of villages, cattle, and gold to their temples. Temple records maintain a log of all the grants it receives from various kings, queens, noblemen, traders, merchants, commoners, devadasis, and other temple employees. Having said that, it can be safely assumed that common persons who could not donate anything worthy of being recorded were also visiting these temples. It is their visits to temples through good and bad times that have kept them alive for the longest time.

Unfortunately, a number of temples in India have been displaced from their original locations—not by choice of either the deities or their devotees. Deities of many temples have had to move to different places due to attacks on temples. Invasions were mounted by foreigners who were against idol worship, as well as by those who had eyes on the immense wealth of these temples. There are thousands of stories of people running away with deities in the middle of the night to shift them to a safer place. Sometimes they swam across rivers to get out of the invaders' territories and sought shelter with neighboring kings or wealthy merchants. Many a time, when carrying away the deities was not an option, they hid them in the depths of wells or riverbeds, where the chances of attacks was minimal. At times, the deities had to be sent underground, buried in pits dug in fields or forests. Where available, they were confined to underground chambers below the temples, out of sight of the eyes seeking to destroy them. New temples were built in safer places where attacks were not expected, at least not in the foreseeable future. The famous Nataraja and Sivakamasundari murtis of Chidambaram had to stay inside the hollow of a tamarind tree for years before returning to their abodes.

Chola bronzes predating the 13th century are showing up every now and then from neatly dug pits, lying face down, as if waiting for their imprisonment to end and return to their shrines, where they would be worshipped and pampered once again. Little do they know of the huge illegal market that has developed for them. Once out of these pits, after passing through hands of smugglers and art dealers, the murtis land up in auction houses. The ones with better luck land up in museums, where the descendants of those who worshipped them can at least see them.

Temples have seen all kinds of days. The premises of the Brihadeeswara Temple in Thanjavur had to serve as an army garrison for European armies during their reign. The whole of the temple belt of Goa in its hinterlands is an example of temples from distant villages huddling together in a safe harbor, protected by a benevolent Hindu king. The architecture of these shifted temples was adapted so as to not stand out as temples. In many parts of the country, the deities stayed in the homes of brahmins who would ensure their regular worship. They stayed indoors, and they traveled incognito—that is, the ones who managed to escape the onslaught.

There are historical records of repeated restoration of many temples by kings who believed in them. The long story of the Vishwanath Temple at Varanasi is little known. Most people believe that it was attacked only by Aurangzeb, who built the Gyan Vapi Mosque at the temple site, and that later, a smaller temple was built closer to the Gyan Vapi well, not too far from the mosque. However, when you look at detailed historical records, you find that it was destroyed many times and rebuilt as many times by different kings. It was first attacked by Qutubudin Aibak in 1194 CE. In the mid-13th century, Razia Sultan—the empress of Delhi—built a mosque there in her name. In the late 16th century, during the reign of Akbar, the temple was reconstructed by Narayan Bhatta with the help of Todar Mal who was a minister in Akbar's court. The 17th century saw another wave of destruction led by Aurangzeb. Dashnami Akhada, a group of warrior sadhus, did put up a fight, but could not save the temple that was converted into the Gyan Vapi Mosque retaining the sculpted walls of the temple. The temple was re-built in the early 18th century and called the Adi Vishveshwara Temple, but it was made to resemble a mosque. The Vishveshwara Linga was moved to the premises of the Avimukteshwara Temple, and over a period of time, the two deities began to be thought of as one and the same. The small temple, as we see it today, was built by Ahilya Bai Holkar, the queen of Malwa in 1777 CE. During all those years when the temple was in shambles, different kings were still visiting it during their Kashi yatra, and there are royal records of this. It can be safely assumed that common pilgrims kept visiting the temple in whatever shape and form it existed during their visits. Just like how layers of paint under the topmost strokes stay invisible to untrained eyes, the efforts of many generations to keep our traditions alive stay invisible to us.

Many of the murtis that were displaced from their original temples have their own tales of arduous journeys to tell. In Nathdwara, you hear the story of Shrinathji coming from Govardhan Parvat in Braj during the Islamic invasions in that region. When you visit Nathdwara, you get lost in the elaborate daily routine of the temple as the whole town revolves around the haveli of Shrinathji. When I first visited Nathdwara, all that the storytellers told me was about how Shrinathji chose this place to live, on his way from Braj. That is all that matters to them. A couple of years later, I got to visit Govardhan Parvat again. Along its twenty-one kilometer parikrama, I stopped at important temples, ponds, and villages on the way, thanks to my young guide Yamini who regaled me with stories of each of these locations. It was then that I saw the original Shrinathji temple at the top of a hill close to Jaitpura village. The temple has a new murti now, but people here never forget that their original deity, their *mool d*evata is in Nathdwara. They believe that he comes here every night and returns to Nathdwara every morning.

Govind Rai Temple is one of the main temples of Jaipur, the temple of the royal family, resplendent in the characteristic pale pink color of the pink city. A small murti of Sri Krishna with an even smaller one of Radha is worshipped here by thousands every day, multiple times a day. I was among these thousands, the day I visited this temple. The delightful color, the painted walls and the peacocks dancing in the gardens next to the temple would stay in my memory for a long time. Little did I know that the murtis worshipped so fondly here originally lived in a beautiful red sandstone temple in Vrindavan that too goes by the same name. The fact that the deity came from Vrindavan is well known in Jaipur but does not get much attention or mention. However, in Vrindavan, they never forget that their original deities are now living in Jaipur. Satisfaction comes from the fact that they are well taken care of by the devotees there. At Vrindavan's Govind Rai

Temple, they will tell you that when Aurangzeb was attacking the land of Krishna for all its temples, Govind Devji was taken to Jaipur. When we view it through a present-day, 21st century lens, we think that this would have happened in a matter of a few hours, for Jaipur is just about two hundred and thirty kilometers away. However, if you were to consider the transportation mechanisms of those days, you would arrive at a journey time of two–three days on a bullock cart, perhaps interspersed with walking trails. It did not even occur to me that Jaipur had not yet been built in the 17th century, when Aurangzeb was attacking all the Hindu temples he could possibly attack and breaking as many murtis as he could. Taking these murtis out to a safe place then must have been the riskiest of tasks. There was a need to protect the deities by keeping them in hiding, even while ensuring that their regular worship took place. Murtis of Govind Devji changed hands multiple times till they reached a safe place in safer times to live peacefully.

Let me just take you through the journey of Govind Devji from his temple in Vrindavan—where the murti was originally installed—to his present temple in the royal precincts of Jaipur, where he is the much revered and loved presiding deity of the city. In 1669 CE, when Aurangazeb was in full form, priests of the Govind Dev Temple first took Govind Devji and Radhaji to Radha Kund, a few kilometers away from the city. Today, Radha Kund is a popular spot full of pilgrims, but in those days, it was surrounded by forests. More importantly, it came under the patronage of the Jat kings. A century before this event, that is, in the mid-16th century, the Gosains of Chaitanya Mahaprabhu had acquired land around Radha Kund when they identified the twin kunds—Radha Kund and Krishna Kund—as sacred kunds for Vaishnavaites. A temporary temple was built for the deities here, but it looked nothing like a temple. It rather resembled an ordinary home. This deviation was made from the prescribed traditions so as to ensure the safety of the deities. In 1671 CE, the deities were moved further inwards to a place called Kaman, away from the Grand Trunk Road that was primarily used by the Mughal armies. The closer you were to the road, the riskier it was to hide and protect the murtis. The deities stayed here for a good four years. People taking care of them were aware of the fact that the deities were there only in transit, until the next move happened. In 1675 CE, they were taken to the Gobindgadha Fort, which is further towards Jaipur. Here, a temple was duly built for them in such a way that it was not visible from outside the fort—it could be seen only on entering the fort. Govind Devji and the other deities stayed here for twenty-five years till 1700 CE. In 1700 CE, they were moved to a village called Khava where they lived for almost seven years till 1707 CE, the year Aurangzeb died. That year, the murtis were moved closer to Jaipur, to a place called Govindapura in Sanganer, where again a temple was built for them, in which they stayed till 1713 CE. For the next two years, the murtis stayed at a place called Kanak Vrindavan near Amer. This was the new Vrindavan built by Sawai Jai Singh as a devotee. In 1715 CE, when the city of Jaipur was still being built, Govind Devji was installed at the Govinda Mahal in the Jainvasa Gardens even before the city was established. This is where he has been living for more than three hundred years now. If we were to count, he traveled through eight transit temples over forty-six years before finding a permanent home at the ninth temple he moved into, at Jaipur. We do not know the minute details of this journey. Scholars have reconstructed this journey based on accounts scattered across different chronicles. Bhagwan only knows how many other stops, detours, hide-outs, and change of hands the journey might have entailed.

The journey of the utsav murtis of Ranganatha ji and Ranganayaki ji of Srirangam, an island banked by the River Kaveri, seems incredible, even though there are records verifying this story. When Malik Kafur attacked

Srirangam in the early 14th century, he destroyed the temple and killed thousands of Vaishnavaites who tried to protect the deities and the temple. The devotees managed to build a wall to protect the main deity, but the invader took away with him to Delhi all the precious utsav murtis from the temple. In Delhi, the sultan's daughter was fascinated by the main utsav murti of Ranganathaswamy. She would play with him. Meanwhile, from Srirangam, the performing troupes of the temple left for Delhi in the hope of bringing back the deities using their skills. They reached Delhi and managed to entertain the sultan of Delhi. When he wanted to reward them, all they asked for were the murtis of Ranganatha ji and Ranganayaki ji. Their wish was granted, and they started traveling back to Srirangam to take the murtis home. The daughter of the sultan got upset when she found her favorite murti missing. The sultan immediately sent his army after the performing troupe to bring back the murti. The troupe members had expected this, and they split themselves in smaller groups and moved in different directions. The group holding the murtis finally managed to hide it below a neem tree, where it stayed for a good sixty years. In the meantime, new murtis were sculpted and installed in the temple. Suddenly, someone found the old Ranganatha murti under the neem tree and brought the murti to Srirangam. Now, the genuine confusion was if this was indeed the real utsav murti of the temple, and how to verify that. An old, blind washerman said he used to have the *tirtham* of the utsav murti in his childhood and could identify it from the taste of its tirtham. "Sure, it is the real utsav murti," he said, after drinking the water used to bathe the newly rediscovered murti. It was duly reinstalled at the temple along with the new one. Then, one day, someone at the temple dreamt of the Ranganayaki murti that was still beneath the same neem tree. The Ranganayaki murti too was retrieved and installed alongside her consort. This makes for a sixty-year exile for these murtis, one that involved travel from Srirangam to

Delhi and back, and living in the forest for the better part of the exile.

Similar journeys can be sketched for many deities that we know—deities who came from place 'A' and now living in place 'B', or those who had been on a long exile before returning home.

We do not even have the count of the deities that are lost forever. Some of them have landed in museums around the world. Do deities belong to museum spaces where they are displayed like a fragment from the past or an artwork, rather than the living beings that they are? Should they be brought back to the temples that were their homes? Do emerging generations of their devotees even identify with the deities as living entities to be worshipped? Have their stories been carefully passed on through successive generations to the current generation? Is someone waiting or yearning for these deities back home, for whom they would return to the temples they once inhabited? Do the temples that housed them still exist, and if they do, do they wait for the deities? Many of the deities must be waiting—in their hide-outs—to be discovered. We do hear of murtis being discovered every now and then, and every time I hear this news, I wonder how many more are still lying buried under the earth's surface. How many of them might we be inadvertently walking upon? Some of these questions will take a few generations of Indians to answer, and perhaps many more to resolve.

The long arduous journeys of these deities tell us as much about their devotees who traveled with them, risking their lives and everything else they had. These stories tell me how much these deities must have meant to society for people to have taken such huge risks. How many of us would think of saving our murtis if we were faced with a barbaric invasion, if being in possession of the murtis would essentially invite death? Many of our ancestors left their homes, but they never left their deities. Society as a whole must have respected the deities, for they were received with respect wherever they stopped, making for another strong case for how delicate threads of tradition bind us together. Temples were built for the deities with whatever was available, in such a way that they were protected. In some cases, it took a few generations to protect these deities and hand them over to the care of future generations.

Today, if the culture surrounding these deities is preserved, it is because of these unknown ancestors of ours who did everything possible in their capacity for the survival of our deities and the traditions associated with them. This understanding made me question the oft-stated statement— "We have survived so many attacks from foreign invaders, we will survive anyhow." These stories made me realize that the survival of our deities and our traditions did not happen on its own. The survival happened because of the sacrifices of so many people. It happened because people valued Indian culture and civilization and they wanted it to be preserved for us.

Incidentally, these tales are known to an exceedingly small circle of people, a fistful of scholars who study these temples, temple records and sculptures academically. They study and publish within their own little world. We hardly read about them in history books, newspapers, magazines, or even in new age media. The snippets that we read hardly tell the whole tale. What is the solution, then?

I would go back to my favorite remedy for all problems— travel. Travel, and you will find that the places speak to you. Walk like a naïve empty cup, willing to take in every story, read every possible sign, and most importantly, connect the dots. The more you experience places first-hand, the more you will start connecting them, based on these invisible threads that connect distant lands with seemingly different cultures, different languages, and different worlds. You will develop an eye for deciphering what is below the surface.

Travel, and with a bit of training in the language of yore, you would not need a mediator to interpret the stories of the past—whatever art and architectural remains you see will tell you their own story, first-hand.

Recreating Sacred Geographies

Many places across India claim to be some version of Kashi. They add it as a suffix to their names, like Uttarkashi or Dakshin Kashi—the reference point being Kashi always, the holiest of places in India. In Karnataka, the Jain temple town of Moodbidari is called the Jain Kashi—indicating that it is the most important pilgrimage place for Jains. Similarly, Ganga gets added to the alternate names of all the rivers of India. In Sri Lanka, the generic word used for rivers is Ganga.

Sometimes, I feel these sacred spaces are taking avatars, and multiplying and projecting themselves so as to be close to a larger number of devotes. On one hand, this helps people who cannot visit distant places for whatever reason, fulfil their desire to visit the pilgrimage place. On the other hand, it helps elevate the sacredness of one's own space by placing it as an equivalent of Kashi or the Ganga.

Classical as well folk literature in India talks extensively about the re-creation of sacred spaces. In fact, in larger tirtha kshetras like Kashi, you find the presence of all the other tirthas and vice-versa. The Mathura Mahatmay in Varah Puran mentions the re-creation of Prayag and the Dashashwamedha Ghat of Kashi in Mathura. The story goes that, they come here, to the sand of Braj, to wash away the sins accumulated from pilgrims throughout the year. Godavari Mahatmay calls Godavari the Dakshin Ganga, thus telling the people living on her banks that they are living on no less sacred a land, nurtured by the Godavari. She is also called *Vriddh* Ganga or the older Ganga, making her more pious than the Ganga descending from the Himalayas, by adding a layer of antiquity. This highlights that while the Ganga was brought to earth by a kshatriya—

King Bhagirath of Ikshvaku dynasty, the Godavari was brought down by a brahmin, Sage Gautama, making her more pious. The Tapi in Central India is also called Suryaputri—daughter of the sun—and is considered older than the Ganga. Her story says that her *tejas* was transferred to the Ganga when she came down to earth, and that is why she continues to have pride of place in the land of Bharata. It is a strange conundrum that while everyone reveres the Ganga and Kashi, they also want to have the same, if not more, pride in the tirthas closer to them.

Kaal Bhairav is a fierce form of Shiva who is also seen as a protector. He is the *nagar kotwal* or the presiding security officer of Kashi, and his small temple can be seen not too far from the Vishwanath Temple. Pilgrimage to Kashi is not considered complete without visiting him. On the west coast of India, there is another Kaal Bhairav temple close to the town of Harihareshwar in Maharashtra. According to a folk story, the Kaal Bhairav of Kashi had to visit the Kaal Bhairav of Harihareshwar. The deal was that he would reach Harihareshwar before the crack of dawn, but due to some reason, he could not keep his word. He managed to reach a place called Shrivardhan, just a few kilometers short of Harihareshwar. A temple was built for him at the same spot, and there, he is now a representative of Kashi's Kaal Bhairav. You can offer the same prayers and ask him for the same boons that you would ask of Kaal Bhairav of Kashi. The import is: There is no need to travel all the way to Kashi; a small Kashi has been built for you, right here, close to you.

You might have heard of different versions of the stories of re-creation of the sacred geographies in your own neighborhood. The idea is to have a piece of that sacred geography close to you, so that you can visit it more often or live close to it.

Come to think of it, all temple *shikharas* or superstructures, especially of the Shiva temples, are essentially trying to replicate the Kailash Parvat. It is a classic example of replication of the space of the deity when you build a home for him in your locality. When the deities have to move to a new location, the same environment is recreated for them in the new location, as we saw in the case of Nathdwara.

From our times, I saw this re-creation at Namchi—a small town in South Sikkim. It is a pilgrimage place called Siddheshwar Dham located on top of the ancient Solophok Hill, believed to be the place where Shiva gave his Pasupatastra to Arjun. A mini India has been re-created here, with all the four dhams, all the twelve Jyotirling temples, and many other important pilgrimage places re-created. Travelers fondly call it the Char Dham, referring to pilgrimage places from across India, which can all be seen here, together. A lesser known kunda, the Satyanarayana Kala Dhamam near Hyderabad, re-creates the different *lokas* or worlds from Indian scriptures in its large campus. Visiting this museum is like watching scriptures come alive.

Does the re-creation of geographies further emphasize the importance of the sacred space that is re-created? Or is it just a convenience created for those who cannot travel too far due to constraints? Travel, after all, was never as easy as it is for us today. People used to travel with almost no contact with their people back home. So, the journey really entailed leaving behind everything one had—family, wealth, society. One could only hope to find it unchanged if and when one came back. Pilgrimages demanded a sound body that could walk unknown paths, a strong will, and a drive that comes only from complete devotion. It was not everyone's cup of tea. Re-creating spaces closer to them was the next best solution, jugaad, if I may say so.

While at one end, the sacred places are replicated in far and distant places, the sacred places they are modelled upon are owned not just by the locals, but by every community that believes in and visits these places regularly. Wander around the streets of Varanasi, and you would find here an imprint of every possible community in the country. Every sect and sub-sect that exists anywhere in India has a representative ashram here. The big ones have their own mathas or ashrams where their followers prefer to stay when visiting Kashi. Even geographically, you would find small regions of India co-existing in this version of a miniature India. There is always a part of Kashi that would feel like home to you. I remember when I first visited Kashi after getting married, everyone in my in-laws' family insisted that I stay in the matha that the family belongs to. They felt it was the safest place to stay, as I was traveling alone, and more importantly, I would get homely food, that you can read as "our kind of food."

My interpretation of this is two-fold. One, in the good old days, the concept of hotels—which, anyone with the right amount of money can access today—did not exist. Nor did there exist the concept of paying guests or guest houses. People opened their homes only to their own relatives and not to strangers. Dharamshalas and ashrams were kind of restricted to the community of their followers. So, if a community wanted to visit and spend some time in the pilgrimage place, they needed a space of their own. Second, food must have been another critical factor. I think, until a few decades ago, most Indians wanted their kind of food. They also wanted fresh, hygienic, and nutritious food, no matter where they were. Dharamshalas, in fact, provide the facility to cook one's own food, for those who stay for longer durations. Even in my childhood, when we visited our kul devi, food that could last for a few days was cooked and packed, so that we do not have to consume outside food. So, every community that has their people regularly visiting places like Kashi or Ujjain or Haridwar would have built their own sanctuaries that would ensure a home for their community in these tirtha *sthalas,* and act as a local support system for their people visiting the place as well. Put together, they create a microcosm of India, making the sacred place as cosmopolitan as possible. Places like Rishikesh and Kainchi Dham of Neem Karoli Baba have extended this concept to world travelers, who visit and live in these places as a community.

If you step back a bit, you realize that the sacred spaces weave India in such a way that, even if you could change its political boundaries, you would not change its spiritual ones. The sacred places bind the geographies by holding so many threads together that, even if a few are lost, some others are still holding on, keeping the spirit alive. At the same time, new threads—that bind us in these times—are busy weaving their wefts and warps. Threads of today will become the cultural past of the future.

Devi and the Roots of Feminism in India

एकैवाहं जगत्यत्र द्वितीया का ममापरा।

—Durga Saptashati 8.5

I am the only one, who else is there apart from me.

Devi or the Divine Feminine is the oldest form of the divine, worshipped in ancient civilizations across the world. The ability to give birth was seen to be divine, and almost all ancient cultures worship mother figures. I am not sure as to how many tribal or aboriginal communities in the world continue to worship mother figures, but I do know for sure that in today's India, devotion to the Devi or the Divine Feminine is as prevalent as devotion to popular male counterparts like Shiva and Vishnu, if not more. How well this has been studied and documented—that feminism in India is rooted in the worship of the Devi—is anybody's guess, though.

My earliest rendezvous with the Devi, aside of visiting Devi temples randomly, was during Kanya Puja or Kanjak as it is called in North India. All of us young girls used to be much in demand on ashtami and navami, or the eighth and the nineth days, of the Chaitra Navaratri that falls in April, and the Sharad Navaratri that roughly falls in early October. All the families in the neighborhood would invite us home. All the uncles, aunties, and their sons—some of whom were our age and hence our friends or classmates—

would wash our feet before making us sit like princesses for the puja. We would be served freshly cooked halwa, puri and black channa. Every home would insist that we eat at least one puri and take some home too. Gifts included a *chunri* or a stole, bangles, sometimes chocolates, or anything else the family wanted to gift us. Some money was given along with the gifts. Everyone in the family bowed down to us and sought our *ashirwad,* our blessings. We obliged. Those were fun times to be a young girl.

There was a naïve sense of self-importance as we knew we were crucial for the puja. The little money that we received was absolutely ours to keep. Our parents would not touch that money. We were asked to keep it with ourselves and spend it on whatever we wanted for ourselves. We all had our lists of what to spend the money on. This money came with absolutely no strings attached, at an age when one is literally dependent on one's parents for all kinds of things. That little money was my first taste of financial freedom and the independence it brings with it.

Decades later, in the era of social media, when celebrations of our festivals is accompanied with an equal dose of condemning of festivals that we do not understand or follow, the topic of Kanya Puja popped up on my twitter timeline. A lady from Kerala, whose religion I could not make out from her name, tweeted on Kanya Puja on ashtami. She tweeted, "North Indians are today, looking for 9 virgin girls (non-menstruating) to feed them food. This is how society lands up paying a premium on virginity and vilifying menstruation." My instant rejoinder was, "Clearly someone who has not been worshipped as Kanya in childhood. You don't feed the Devi, you seek her blessings. Hope you get in touch with the Devi that resides inside you, the Shakti that is within you!"

I do not generally get into arguments with activists of any kind on social media, and definitely not with the professional clickbait outraging industry. But this rejoinder just jumped out from somewhere inside me. It took me a few days to understand that it was rooted in my childhood when I was worshipped as a kanya.

The ritual of Kanya Puja subconsciously told me that I may be a small girl, frail in comparison to those who were worshipping me, I may be dependent on them in every possible way, for people worshipping us included our own families, but I still had something to give them, something that they seek by way of this puja. It connected me with the 'power of giving' that resides inside me. Hopefully, it also told those worshipping us during Navaratri that there is a Devi inside every little girl whom you must respect. It was a day when power equations got reversed. Today, I feel this puja also let me imbibe the knowledge that the Devi is within me, that I am the Devi, with all her powers.

Years later, I would read the Devi Bhagwat and learn about the rituals prescribed for Kanya Puja. It talks of worshipping girls aged between two and ten years as kanyas. It elaborates the different *swaroops*, the manifestations, that a girl takes each year, during this period of her life. A one-year-old girl is too young, as her faculty of smell is not yet developed, and after ten years of age, it is assumed that she starts menstruating, so she is not a kanya anymore. In case a girl starts menstruating, she ceases to be a kanya even if she is ten years old or younger. From the age of two to ten years, a girl takes nine different swaroops, and most homes worship nine kanyas during Navaratri, celebrating the nine forms the Devi takes during these nine auspicious days. Now, modern-day feminists may argue that this is discrimination based on menstruation. I would argue that the beginning of menstruation is a transformation from being a girl to a woman, post which you are not worshipped as kanya, but you take other forms of the Devi. When you get married, which essentially would be after you start menstruating, you enter your marital home as Lakshmi. You participate in many rituals like Haldi-Kumkum or Var

Lakshmi Puja, wherein you are worshipped as Lakshmi swaroop or the manifestation of Lakshmi.

I saw another beautiful variation of revering young girls as kanyas or Devi swaroop at the Kumbh Mela. A young *nati* was walking on a tightrope, holding a stick in her hands. I have seen such acts on television, but watching it on the mela grounds in the middle of thousands of people was another experience. My heartbeats kept pace with her feet, I worried for her every time she took a step on the rope and I breathed a sigh of relief when she reached the other end safely and sat on the 'V' of the pole to which the rope was tied. People paid whatever they felt like or could afford. Suddenly, I saw people walk up to the girl, touch her feet, and seek her blessings. Some even went to the extent of touching her feet with their foreheads. The reaction of the young nati told me that she was used to this. This was not a part of any formal ritual; this was not needed as the girl and her family did this as a profession, but nevertheless, people saw the divine energy in her skill and courage to walk on the tightrope. They saw the Devi in her, paid their respects and sought her blessings.

Are these rituals and behaviors really a way of giving regular reminders that the Devi is inside you, that you are a Devi? In fact, in the Devi Mahatmay from the Markandeya Puran, a prime Shakta text, the Devi tells an asura, "I am every woman." We just need to remember this.

I was at the Mangala Devi Temple in Mangalore when I learnt that the city is named after her. Mangaluru in Kannada literally means the home of Mangala. She is the presiding deity of the city. It reminded me of the fact that Chandigarh, the city where I have spent many of my growing up years, is named after Chandi Devi, whose temple I have somehow never managed to visit, even though I studied in the army cantonment area called Chandimandir. This train of thoughts added Kolkata, Mumbai, Durgapur, and Srinagar to the series. In a moment of inquiry, on a weekend, I posted this as a question on my social media handle: Tell me the names of Indian cities named after the Devi. I did not expect more than ten to fifteen names, I would have been happy to receive fifteen odd names. However, by the end of two days, I had a list of fifty plus names—most of them were well known cities like Shimla, Ambala, Kanyakumari and Tarapur. Even Bangladesh's capital Dhaka, I discovered, is named after Dhakeshwari Devi. I learnt that the city of Mirzapur is actually Meerjapur, meaning the city of the one born from the ocean, who is none other than Lakshmi. I found this difficult to believe, and someone on twitter duly gave me an official document to prove it. A year down the line, I would visit the city and found that it was indeed written as Meerjapur in all official records.

I published the list from this fun exercise on my travel blog and more names started adding up. I plotted these cities on the map of the Indian subcontinent and what emerged was an all-pervasive footprint of the Devi across the country. All this while, I was aware of the fact that we had not yet included many villages that are named after their *gram* devis or the presiding devis of the respective villages. Even a city like Mumbai has many localities named after the gram devis of the villages which are now a part of the metropolis. In a year after publishing this post, I presented this as a crowdsourced study at two conferences—one at a conference on Shakti worship in India at Amrita University in Kerala, and the other at the Prakriti Parva at Indira Gandhi National Center for Arts in New Delhi. Every time I presented it to a galaxy of scholars, I saw them as surprised and awestruck as I was when I first compiled the list. A lot more needs to be studied on this is what everyone opined. I agree and continue to research on this in my individual capacity.

When some people suggested that I add the cities surrounding the Shaktipeethas to this list, I realized that none of the cities already in my list were Shaktipeethas that define the sacred geography of the Indian subcontinent by their geographical setting. So, if we superimpose the two maps—the map of places in India named after the Devi, and the map of the Shaktipeethas, what we would see is an all-pervading Devi footprint in India.

On and off, when I see this post, I wonder why this obvious pattern has not caught our eyes and escaped our minds for so long. Is it the nature of the Shakti to stay behind and appear only when she is sought? Does her inherent strength remain hidden until it needs to be used or displayed? I am reminded of my visit to the Rukmini Temple in Dwarka that stands on the outskirts of the town. At her temple, even today, you can get a copy of the letter that she had written to Sri Krishna asking him to abduct and marry her. The letter continues to be read every day at the temple of Dwarkadhish, at night, just before Sri Krishna retires for the day. At Rukmini Temple, young women who want to get married read out this letter so that their soulmates reach out to them, just as Krishna reached out to Rukmini's call. I picked up a copy of the letter from the temple purohit. It is one of my prized possessions now, even though the text is easily available online with a simple google search.

Rukmini Temple in Dwarka

The story goes that Rukmini was about to be married to Shishupal—the king of Chedi, which would be the area around Bhubaneshwar today. Rukmini was the daughter of the king of Vidarbha, the area around modern-day Nagpur. Sri Krishna was in his Dwarka, on the western edge of India overlooking the Arabian Sea. Rukmini had never met Krishna, she had only heard about him and fallen in love with him based on what she had heard. Even if she had seen Krishna—as per some accounts—there was never a meeting between the two. She is determined to marry him despite the fact that her father had decided and made arrangements for her to be married to someone else. Marriages in royal families are political affairs and the fates of kingdoms are built around them. Rukmini clearly understands this. Despite this, she is determined to marry Krishna. She writes a letter in exactly seven shlokas communicating her love for him, her commitment to him, and about how, when and where he can reach her, abduct her, and take her along with him. I have often said that this letter is a great example of how to communicate effectively. Consider this scenario: You have not met the person, you have no existing relationship with the person, you do not even know if he knows anything about you, but you want him to not just listen to you, but also to do exactly what you tell him to do and achieve the desired result. You need to be precise as there is no time for elaborations. We don't know if Rukmini wrote down the verses, or made the brahmin who carried this message memorize these shlokas. In either case, brevity was essential. The letter told Krishna that she would be relatively alone when she visits the Girija Devi Temple as part of the wedding rituals, a day before her proposed wedding, and that was the best opportunity to abduct her. Krishna follows her words and abducts her from the temple.

Rukmini's courage and conviction come through in her letter. Generally, we do not hear too much about her. The act of her marriage usually gets attributed as a courageous act of Krishna, as he abducted her to fulfil her wish. However, when you read this letter, you know it is Rukmini's wish, her desire, her conviction, her plan, and her desired outcome. Krishna was just doing what she wanted him to do, even before they ever met and way before they got married.

I must admit I am totally fascinated by this letter. The more I reflect on it, more layers reveal themselves. At one level, it tells me about the inherent nature of women in India. They have all the strength, but they choose to stay in the background. If you really look at your homes, you will know that it is the lady of the house who really takes a whole lot of decisions. However, they make it look as if the man is in charge. The imprint of the woman in the decision is always there, though it may not be there in its communication to the larger world. This reminds me of a WhatsApp forward: A man may be the head of the family, but the woman is the neck who gets to decide which way the head turns.

Cultural nuances hidden within the language employed by the characters in our epics convey the same. For example, in an episode of Ramayana as mentioned in the Devi Bhagwat, where Sita *haran* or the abduction of Sita is being described, Ravana introduces himself to Sita as Sriman Mandodari Pati, the husband of Mandodari, and Lankesh, the ruler of Lanka. Does it not convey that Mandodari was as well-known as her husband, if not more? Despite the image we have of Ravana as an alpha male abductor, he had no qualms in introducing himself with reference to his chief queen, even if it was with the intention to attract Sita by telling her that she could be in the place of Mandodari. Throughout the retellings of the Ramayana, Sita is referred as Janaksuta, Janaki, Vaidehi, and of course Rampriya. Ram is often called Janakivallabha, meaning someone dear to Janaki or Janaksutvaram, meaning the husband of the daughter of Janak, or some other name that identifies him through Sita. Nowhere do I see Sita being introduced as Dashrath's or Kaushalya's daughter-in-law, or as Mrs. Suryavanshi. I am yet to find a similar example in our modern-day literature, even in those texts that intend to bring in so-called gender equality. The irony is that, in this same land, today, women change their names after marriage in a way that they lose their pre-marital identity. We do not seem to have a historical basis for this practice. Women used to pretty much stay as their father's daughters or the daughters of the lands they were born in. Most queens in our epics are identified more by their birthplace than by their real names; think of Gandhari—princess of Gandhar, Panchali—daughter of Panchal, and Madri—daughter of Madradesh. Even in our families, we often distinguish between our relatives based on their place of residence—*Kanpur wale chacha* or *Rishikesh wali bua.*

At Shekhawati, in the opulent *havelis* or mansions of rich merchants of the previous century, there is a room called '*baithak*' where all the business meetings used to take place. On the face of it, only men participated in the meetings; but there were *jharokhas* or windows for the women of the house to listen in to these conversations. Men in the house would always consult the women on key business decisions. Coming from a business community, I can see this happening in almost all traditional business families. The prime responsibility of women may be managing the home, but they do have their opinion on the business dealings that are conducted by their husbands and other male members of the family. I remember a prominent businessman in my extended family, who passed away suddenly, in his early forties. Until then, his wife had focused on managing their three children, and at best had helped organize business parties. However, once this mishap occurred, soon after the rituals were over, she took over the business and ran it without any interruption, training, or any formal handover. I would later discover many such examples in business families. Is this how women in India lived in the past, as a source of strength to the family, as its heart and mind, but choosing to stay in the background. Since the whole family was regarded as one unit, no one really bothered to divide and distribute the credit or any other returns that came with the decision.

Today, like the Devi in each home, Devi temples too are out there, everywhere, and wield their influence on the world, though we often tend to lose sight of them. They are there, all over the country, in every city, in every village and on its outskirts, on hilltops, in the fifty-one or 108 Shaktipeethas, and in the places named after them; but you see them only when you actively seek them. For example, when you visit Pushkar, most people visit the Brahma Temple and the famous Pushkar lake but only a seeker goes and visits the Manibandh Shaktipeetha in the city. Apparently, just as it is in our individual lives, Devi is always there and playing her role in the wider universe, it is we who sometimes forget to acknowledge her.

Haridwar is a popular pilgrim destination. Most of the time, people visit Haridwar to take a dip in the Ganga and participate in the famous Ganga Arti at Har ki Paudi, and come back. Those with some time on their hands may visit the popular Mansa Devi and Chandi temples located on the two hills surrounding the city. How many of us realize that Haridwar is a prime Devi kshetra? Most of us do not know of Maya Devi, who is the presiding deity of this city, after whom the city was originally called Mayapur. It is the place where the epochal story of the Shaktipeethas originated when Sati immolated herself.

Shaktipeethas are the places where Sati's body parts fell when they were cut by Vishnu using his Sudarshan Chakra. There are various versions you hear regarding the number of Shaktipeethas that exist across India – they vary anywhere from four to 108. The popular versions include eighteen that Adi Shankaracharya's verses mention, fifty-one as defined in the Tantrachudamani, or 108 as defined in the Devi Bhagwat and the Matsya Puran. The Tripura Rahasya has a list of twelve important devi kshetras. No two lists agree with each other. No smaller list is an absolute subset of the larger list. It seems like different sets of devotees have their own version regarding the number of devi temples in India. Perhaps, these lists were compiled at different points in time in history. If we make a 21st century list, we may come out with an entirely different list.

What I found interesting during my travels is that even when it comes to the Shaktipeethas that feature in all the lists, when you actually reach that place, there may be more than one temple claiming to be the Shaktipeetha. I saw this at many places. Lalita Devi Shaktipeetha, where the fingers of Devi Sati had fallen is said to be in Prayag, and it features in almost all lists of Shaktipeethas. When I was in Prayagraj for the Kumbh Mela, I devoted a day to explore the devi temples of Prayag. My first stop was a tiny temple in pale pink color—Alopi Devi Mandir—where there is no deity but only a *jhoola* or swing hanging over a well. *Alopi* means the one who vanishes. So, the absence of any physical form of the deity here is understandable. Purohits at this temple tell you that this is the Prayag Shaktipeetha. As I walked around the temple on the cold January morning, I saw several people sitting and doing their *sadhna,* or reading the Devi Mahatymay—a key Shakta text. I next visited the Lalita Devi Temple located some distance away from the Alopi Devi Temple. Now, this temple is called the Lalita Devi Temple, which implies a high probability of it being the Shaktipeetha of that region. It is a small temple that looks fairly new, but then, living temples undergo renovations all the time. The temple has a composite image of the three Devis, just like many other devi temples in Uttar Pradesh. The wall adjacent to the sanctum is fully covered by Sri Yantras. The purohit here told me that this was the Lalita Shaktipeeth mentioned in the scriptures. Close to the Lalita Devi Temple is another devi temple called the Lalita Kalyani Temple. Built in an old haveli style, the temple quotes the puranas on its walls, telling you that this is indeed the Shaktipeetha of Prayag. The purohit of the temple shared that the thirty-two *ungal* or thirty-two-fingers-tall original murti is hidden behind the metal cover that most visitors see, and how it is exactly the way the puranas describe it. According to them, the Shaktipeetha of Prayag is Lalita Kalyani and not just Lalita. Can there ever be a consensus on this? I doubt it. Does it matter? Honestly, no. Having visited all of them, I can only say which one feels the most ancient, or the one where I sense the strongest energy field of the Devi. When I say this, I am well aware that the answers for this too would differ from person to person. As they say, to each his own.

All this confusion and contradictions do not really deter the people who believe in the Shakti of these temples in any way. People who follow Shakta traditions would visit the temples of their chosen Devi swaroop. They are inherently aware of the fact that all these are manifestations of the same Devi. Different manifestations only recall the different acts performed by the Devi, like the killing of a particular asura. Mahishasurmardini gets her name for killing Mahishasur, Mumba Devi for killing Mumbarak asura and Kolhapur Mahalakshmi is known for killing Kolhasur, who lends his name to the city she lived in—Kolhapur. I will try to explain this with an analogy. Today, a woman may be a mother, a wife, a professional, a hobbyist, and a fitness enthusiast— among the many roles that she plays in life. To her children, her primary role is that of a mother; everything else takes a backseat, though it does not disappear. To her team at work, her primary role is that of a professional who is responsible for delivering certain goals for the organization; her personal roles takes a backseat for these people, they may or may not be aware of her other roles.

For her hobby mates, say, if her hobby is photography, she is just a photographer judged on the quality of the images she creates. Effectively, she is one person playing multiple roles, and she is more than the sum of all the parts she is playing. However, different people relate to different aspects of her. Actually, this applies to all of us—men and women. This is much the same way we relate to a particular aspect of the Devi; she is more than the sum of all the manifestations she takes in our universe. A devotee is aware of this, and he is also aware of the fact that it is not easy to understand the all-encompassing nature of Shakti. He may choose the aspect of Devi Shakti that he has inherited through his family or his lineage of gurus; or he may choose the swaroop that appeals to him, the Shakti that he connects with, based on his instinct.

A fascinating aspect of devi temples, I found, was that many of them exist on hill tops on the outskirts of inhabited areas; even today, we still have to trek to reach most of these devi temples. Some famous ones have got steps leading up to them, and some famous ones have cable cars taking you to the temple. For example, all the hills surrounding the Pushkar Lake and town have devi temples on the hills. The famous Savitri Devi Temple has a broad stairway leading to the temple, and a cable car option too. On the other hand, Manibandh or the Manivedika Devi Temple on the adjacent hill has a small representative temple built at the base of the hill for the ease of the pilgrims. The Ekadashi or Papmochini Mata Temple sits on another hilltop nearby and can be accessed only by trekking up the steep hill. Similarly, the Pavagadh Hill in Gujarat is full of ancient Hindu and Jain temples and medieval monuments, and atop this hill is the most ancient Kalika Devi Temple. This is probably the oldest temple on this hill, and everything else would have come up later. Even today, during Navaratri, you can see many devotees trek up the hill to reach the temple. I used the cable car to visit the temple, but still, I had to climb the steep last leg of the journey.

Other places where you are most likely to find devi temples are at ancient forts. Somewhere in the middle of the ruins of ancient forts, you often find their only living entities to be the devi temples, like I found at Kapilvastu in Nepal. Kapilvastu, as you know, was the capital of Sudhodhan, the father of Gautam Buddha. It was in this palace that Gautam spent the first twenty-nine years of his life, and when he stepped out, he really stepped out to figure out the world. The 2300 plus-year-old fort palace is in absolute ruin. You can barely see the outline of the palaces, and the only intact structures are the stupas of Buddha's parents. The temple of Samay Devi in the premises is the only surviving living space. You see a series of elephant figures—from miniatures to those that are a few feet tall—surrounding the temple. Here, the Devi continues to live, even while those who installed her have perished ages ago. I saw the same pattern in many forts in India.

Devi, in one or the other forms, is the Aradhya or the patron deity of warrior clans and used to be worshipped before going on war. For a long time, I wondered why the Devi is the patron deity of warrior clans, and why she is worshipped before going to war. After reading a few Shakta texts, I realize that no one has won as many battles as she has. In fact, in most big battles, when everyone else has lost or given up, the final lap of these wars was fought and won by the Devi for the righteous. The biggest of asuras were killed by her single-handedly, or with the help of her army of *yoginis* and her manifestations like the Sapta Matrikas.

Reading the Devi Mahatmay told me about the Shakti or the power that women have. I wonder—in a land that has deities like Mahakali, when did we start believing that women are weak, dependent, docile and must be taken care of? When did women start thinking of themselves as victims, when they have the power to win the biggest battles ever?

I was at the Rani ki Vav in Patan, which can be an overwhelming experience for anyone who appreciates architecture and ornate sculptures. When you walk down the stepwell's seven beautiful levels beneath the ground level, leading to a well where all the water must have collected, you cannot but admire the engineering acumen of our ancestors. They not only understood the need to conserve every drop of water for survival in relatively dry places, but they built these stunningly beautiful stepwells that mesmerize you even in their ruins. I wondered if the exquisite beauty of the sculptures at Rani ki Vav owes to the fact that this stepwell was built by a woman—Rani Udaymati. It is said that she built it in the memory of her husband. What a lovely approach to building a memorial! This is one that is not just beautiful, but also serves the most basic needs of the public. Walking through the Rani ki Vav, I was looking for the bust of Rani Udaymati; as per my research, this used to exist at the stepwell. However, I could not find it either at the site or at the museum next door; but it made me contemplate about the monuments that women have built in India.

I came home and started looking back at my own travels to find such monuments, and I was in for a surprise. Many prominent monuments and temples have been built by queens or wealthy women who funded them from their personal incomes. What also stood out was that, when women built these monuments, they did it either in memory of their loved ones, as a gesture of gratitude for what they have received, or for a larger public good. For example, Avabai, the wife of the famous Mumbai-based Parsi businessman Jamshetjee Jejeebhoy, built the Mahim Causeway when her wish to have a daughter was fulfilled. A thread of this thought led me to Rani Rashmoni of Bengal, who built the famous Dakshineshwar Kali Temple based on a dream she had had on her Kashi Yatra. In fact, many temples were built by queens of big and small kingdoms, it is just that we do not have documentation highlighting this.

When I travel around pilgrimage sites in India, the imprint of Rani Ahilya Bai Holkar is impossible to miss. She single-handedly funded the reconstruction and conservation of so many temples that were destroyed and needed conservation. Every important temple from Kashi Vishwanath to Vishnupad at Gaya to ghats in Haridwar to temples in Maharashtra has her imprint. She either rebuilt them or added something to them. Ghats and stepwells were also her focus, alongside temples. When I stayed at her simple wooden palace right next to the loveliest riverfront in India, at Maheshwar overlooking the Narmada River, I wondered where her strength came from. Her life-size diorama in her *rajwada*, the setting where she met her ministers and the public, holding the Shivalinga in her hands and wearing a simple white sari brings you face-to-face with the inner strength of the woman. I read her biography to know more about her life and work, and what I came across was a life that had seen more challenges than most of us can ever imagine. I was struck by how, even way back in the 18th century, how well connected she had been with the rest of India to be able to carry out construction and conservation activities across the country, even if it was primarily by way of funding. Did she have a lot of funds at her disposal? I do not think so. She chose to use her funds wisely for public works, rather than live in luxury. What drove her was a sense of responsibility to run the kingdom as efficiently as her father-in-law had trained her to, and her deep desire to serve the public. It was her dharma that drove her to do in one lifetime what most of us would take many lifetimes to even think about. When I slept in the simple room of Ahilya Fort overlooking the Narmada, which she had probably used, I just hoped that her spirit will inspire many more men and women to follow her footsteps.

During my travels, I often meet groups of women traveling on their own—such as women walking along the Narmada River for the Narmada Parikrama, or a bunch of them sitting in the courtyard of Dwarkadhish Temple in Dwarka early in the morning, singing bhajans, as they wait for the Makhan Mishri prasad to be distributed. Conversations with them are fun and insightful. They travel with a sense of camaraderie, in a playful mood, out to live for themselves away from all their responsibilities and worries. I often see them laughing and smiling as they interact among themselves or with fellow travelers. I imagine them going back home after their travels and narrating the stories of these places to their grandchildren just like my dadi did. I hope they will collect the India stories from nooks and corners of the country away from their own homes and take them back home to youngsters in their families. I hope they will tell them about the common wealth that we have scattered around this country, that we must care for and enjoy.

These traveling groups of women tell me that women in this country have always been traveling, alone or in groups, with family, with friends and even with strangers. They know how to walk on this land, independently as well as with others. It is just that they never carried a placard of being solo-travelers and they do not make sensational media stories. They themselves do not think they are being extraordinary. For them, it is a journey, a quest, a yatra that they must go on, mostly when they have taken care of their prime responsibilities back home. To me, they all are walking-talking devis, they inspire me, and they are my soul sisters whom I meet on every ancient pilgrimage paths. Nothing satisfies me more than the fact that I am one them.

Heritage through the Lens of Engineering

एतत यंत्राणनूरुपेण कुर्यात प्रासादमुत्ताम्मम ।
यन्त्रविकल्पभेदेन कीर्तिः जायते निष्फला ॥

—Shilpa Prakasha

Temples must be built in accordance with the yantra, the ones that deviate from the yantra bear no fruit or do not work properly.

At the Thiruketeswarar Temple in Sri Lanka, I was talking to sthapati Selvaraj and his wife Ponni who were working on the temple's expansion that was underway then, one of the many phases of expansion the temple has seen. I spent two days with them, learning about the temple's architecture and how they work on expanding an already existing temple structure, and observing the nuances of stone carving. I saw how the stones get marked using a thread soaked in red pigment serving as a straight-line marker, and how each stone is chiseled. Out of sheer curiosity, I tried my hands at chipping off a piece of stone under the expert guidance of the sthapati. One of the things I learnt was, if you hold the chisel at a right angle, chipping away at a stone is easier than it seems. Of course, it would take a lifetime to learn the right angles to hold the tools. Nevertheless, these were two of the most enriching days of my life. I may have visited hundreds of temples, but none of it has given me as much insight into the principles of vaastu shastra and shilpa shastra as this visit did. Even among scholars of temple architecture who focus on interpreting sculptures and their styles, how sculptures are actually created is rarely spoken about. This knowledge stays with the sthapati community who inherit it from their families and gurus.

As we walked through the grey stone being worked upon by the team of sculptors and were in different stages of workmanship, sthapati Selvaraj tapped some of the stones and demonstrated to me the variations in the stones based on the sounds they produce. He went on to elaborate on the different kinds of stones that are used to make different kinds of murtis. Apparently, there are different ways of classifying stones, including assigning them a gender. Yes, there are male stones, female stones, and neutral stones. Shilpa shastra texts precisely prescribe the use of each of these stones while building a temple. I was still absorbing this nuance when I was told about the *navpashan*—an amalgamation of nine types of minerals that has been used for a murti of Karthikeyan at Palani in Tamil Nadu. I quizzed them on how they identify and source the stones, and they simply attributed it to training with senior sthapatis.

Sitting at the guest house behind the temple, Ponni ji walked me through the four different types of maintenance routines that our scriptures prescribe for temples. This includes regular maintenance that must be done once every twelve years for practicing temples, regular expansion of the temples in adherence to the original dimensions and plan of the temple, restarting temple rituals and worship at temples that have fallen out of use for some reason, and cleansing the temples that have been deliberately desecrated.

Now, I found it interesting how the expansion plans of a temple are mandated to follow the dimensions set by the original architect. I was walked through the concept of a base square unit that is used for a temple and is always replicated in multiples. So, if the base unit is one square feet, all the enclosures would be in multiples of this unit while building the temple, and also while expanding it. It is this base unit that replicates and gives symmetry, and eventually rhythm, to the temple. It is also the key that future architects must follow to maintain the sacred architecture of the temple. Think of it as building with just cubes or Lego blocks that have the same length on each side—blocks of exactly the same size. You cannot cut or alter the cubical pieces, but you can pick and use as many such blocks as you can afford to, to modify the temple.

Much later, I would hear Dr. R. N. Iyengar, who has translated the Narada Shilpashastra, talk about this base unit and how it is hidden within the structure of the temple for subsequent generations to decipher. He demonstrates this with the example of the Konark Sun Temple in one of his talks. Similarly, glimpses of our advanced engineering heritage can be seen in the town planning of Sindhu Saraswati Civilization sites like Harappa, Dholavira and Rakhigarhi. In all these well laid out towns, we see the same idea of using a base square unit to plan the town as well its major buildings.

In the several hours of my conversation with the sthapati couple, the lens through which I view temples got one more filter added to it—engineering. I came to know about the various scriptures that give precise details of how temples should be built, what kind of site should be selected, how the temple's dimensions should be decided, what material should be used for what purpose, and how the temple comes alive once the pran pratishtha of the deity is done by opening the deity's eyes. What is fascinating is that, all these rules and prescriptions still leave space for the creativity of the architects and sculptors, especially when it comes to the styles and the stories that are told through the sculptures on the walls. This is what makes each temple unique. We usually get lost in the beautiful sculptures and the grand scales of the massive temples, and often, what remains invisible to the casual eye is the sheer engineering genius that has kept these temples standing for thousands of years. Basic common sense tells us that all this could not have been done without extensive knowledge of soil, stones, and other material, and without a comprehensive understanding of the kind of foundations needed for these massive structures to stand firm.

The view through this lens made me zoom in on some of the engineering marvels of India that I have visited. I collated them into a post on my blog and the response to it reenforced the fact that, like me, most people miss out on the engineering angle when they look at our ancient heritage.

Kailash Temple Ellora

The greatest engineering marvel of India across ages, in my opinion, is the Kailasa Temple or Cave No. 16 of the UNESCO world heritage site of the Ellora Caves near Aurangabad. This temple has been carved top down out of a monolithic volcanic basalt rock. How precise must have been the vision of the architect who visualized this spectacular and intricate temple inside a large, solid block of rock! To chisel away what is not needed, knowing that any mistake could not be corrected and would remain forever, is nothing less than sheer genius. The temple with its giant elephants is impressive from any angle you look at it. My favorite view is the one from the first floor, wherein you see its architecture from an aerial view. The massive stone roof hanging over the temple's corridors always makes me marvel at the precise knowledge our ancient architects must have had of the load-bearing capacity of the pillars they carved beneath the roof. It would have required a precise plan and impeccable knowledge of the nature of the hard rock that was to be chiseled. Come to think of it, today, we just cannot even recreate this masterpiece, even with all the new-age technology available to us.

Chand Baori at Abhaneri in Rajasthan

When we look at Rani ki Vav, the magnificent seven-story stepwell beneath the ground in Patan, again, we tend to get lost in the beauty of the stunning sculptures that adorn its walls at all levels. We forget that the stepwell has stayed intact with all its stone pillars, steps and walls standing solid, even after a good thousand years. A stepwell of this scale and grandeur could not have been built without a deep understanding of geoscience, the pressure that would be exerted on this underground structure, and the strength the stone pillars would need to have to withstand this pressure. The site must have been chosen based on the availability of ground water, along with factors such as the capacity of the soil to hold water. At the same time, it had to be accessible to the general public for safely using the water tapped in it. The beauty of this stepwell enthralls you when you stand on any of its levels and look at its ornate well at the bottom. Our senses are engaged completely by its beauty that it does not occur to us that every level would have been dug up with precise calculations, and that the stepwell must have been designed with precise inbuilt specifications which has bestowed sturdy longevity to it, despite it lying in total neglect for a very long time. The same goes for all the stepwells we see across the country, to varying extents, be it the photogenic Chand Baori at Abhaneri or the Pushkarni at Hampi in Karnataka, or the Agrasen Baoli right in the heart of Delhi. The depth of the stepwell indicates the level of water in the surrounding area. The deeper it is, the lower is the average level of water below the ground, in that area. No wonder that in drier areas like Patan in Gujarat, you find that stepwells go far deeper than the ones you see in South India.

Likewise, large man-made ponds like Surajkund on the outskirts of Delhi—incidentally, this pond is better known for its annual crafts mela—were created to manage uninterrupted water supply for human habitations around them. In the Surajkund pond, you see steps leading down to the water surface, and even ramps for animals to walk upon and drink the water.

Shringaverpur near Prayagraj—that gets a mention in the Ramayana as the place where Sri Ram, Lakshman and

Sita crossed the Ganga— encapsulates another brilliant ancient water management system. The Ganga swells during monsoons, causing a flood-like situation in Uttar Pradesh and Bihar. At Shringaverpur, a series of canals connected to tanks take the excess water of Ganga to a silting tank that allows the dust particles in the water to settle down. From here, it passes through a series of stepped inlets that further cleanses the water, and relatively clean water reaches the final tank from where it is used for human consumption. If the water exceeded the capacity of this tank, there was a provision to send the excess water back to River Ganga. What a beautiful way to draw water from the river when she has excess water and return it back to her when you have more than what you need! And all this is made to happen automatically, through an inbuilt mechanism. Should this not be our inspiration when we design our water storage projects?

At the Kanheri Caves located in the middle of the Sanjay Gandhi National Park in Mumbai, we look at the rock-cut caves, marveling at the beautifully carved stories of the Buddha and the Bodhisattvas. As we move from cave to cave, we inadvertently cross water channels that connect the different water tanks present at different levels throughout the caves. Not many of us perceive that this must have been the lifeline of the ancient cave dwellers who lived here. This interlinked system of tanks and water channels works so well that each drop of rainwater falling on the surface collects in the highest tank. Once it is full, the overflowing water is channelized to the next tank, and so on. Channels carved inside these caves along the walls join the channels outside. It does not stop here. The channels have been carved in a way that the cave entrances always stay dry, or at least do not get flooded when it rains. Contrast this with the flooding we see in our cities as soon as it starts raining, every year, and year after year—the worst of it happening in the same city of Mumbai! Where, when, and why did we let go of our traditional knowledge while planning and building our cities? Did our mindless copying of western principles, that were probably relevant for their weather and water conditions, betray us?

The best illustration of water management, of course, is at Mandu, an ancient city that is located atop a tabletop hill, surrounded by beautiful valleys all around. The place has no source of groundwater whatsoever, and the closest river is also too far away to lend any of her water. Here, every drop of rainwater is captured in tanks, lakes and stepwells built at different levels. Every building here is built around a water body, including the palaces and watchtowers. Every structure here is in some way a water collection contrivance. When you walk on the roads here, a water body is never out of sight. Mandu was one of the most densely populated places in the world once upon a time, and it was totally self-sufficient as far as water was concerned, thanks to the water management technology it utilized to the hilt. When you look at the swimming pools and fountains in its palaces, you realize that luxuries do not come from having abundance, but from managing what you have well.

I must mention the terracotta pipelines that I saw at the ancient city of Petra in Jordan. Located in the middle of the desert, it seems the city was well equipped to collect all of the six inches of rainwater it receives through the year, and purify it naturally for the city to thrive on for a long time. This is one of the first things I noticed when I was walking through the Siq—a natural parting of rocks that leads to the famous treasury of Petra. One side of Siq is lined with terracotta pipes and the other with limestone channels to channel water through the city, with a clear demarcation between drinking water and water for other kinds of use. Here again, most people marvel at the rock shelters and the carved facades of the tombs and monasteries, but often miss taking cognizance of Petra's crucial water management system which would have been the first requirement for the people who made it their home. Apparently, we are not alone in ignoring our ancient engineering heritage.

Hydraulic engineering finds its oldest ancestors in the waterworks of the Sindhu Saraswati Civilization, which did have mechanisms to push water upwards. Some of it can be seen at Dholavira. This would have contributed to many advancements in the famed civic life of this civilization.

Many old temples in India have been built far from the source of the stones used to build them. From my various readings, it seems like rivers were used to transport heavy stones from one part of the country to another. We do know that the Ashoka pillars currently in Delhi were transported during medieval times on the waters of the Yamuna River, from Topara Kalan near Yamunanagar in Haryana and from Meerut in Western Uttar Pradesh. There is documentation of the pillars being wound with silk ropes while they were being uprooted from their original place, properly packed thereafter with cotton to avoid damage, and then transported on carts with as many as forty-two wheels, using capstans and pulleys to load and unload. Transportation between the cities happened on large boats that were ferried on the Yamuna River.

How did the large blocks of stone for temples reach the nooks and corners of the Indian subcontinent from the quarries of Chunar near Varanasi and Mathura? It is still a mystery. It seems, for constructing the Konark Sun Temple, special canals were built to transport the stones to the temple site. Not just stones, even humans traveled on such waterways in ancient India. The Sindhu Saraswati Valley seals depict different types of boats used for transportation, which must have docked at ports like Lothal.

On a related note, we all feel awed by the travels of Adi Shankaracharya, who in his twenty-four years of travel left a footprint in every part of India, debating, discussing, and setting up institutions. He too traveled primarily on waterways. So, besides nurturing us with their waters, rivers have also been our paramount mode of transport since time immemorial, letting us reach countries far and near, and independent of a fuel source, at that. Is this one of the reasons we began to worship our rivers?

At the incomplete Shiva Temple at Bhojpur near Bhopal, we see a ramp that is believed to have been used to take stones to the higher levels of the structure, especially the huge single stones like the Amalaka that sits atop the tall temple shikharas. In the good old days, they probably used the strength of elephants to lug the stones up the ramp. Even so, it still intrigues me how they managed to take the last of the needed stones up the shikara, when a silly mistake could have destroyed the delicate carvings on the structure beneath. I am yet to find an answer to this.

The hill monasteries of Ladakh, Lahual and Spiti valley in the cold desert region of the Himalayas are a wonder in themselves. The fragile Dhanker Monastery appears to be hanging from a cliff. The giant Key Monastery sits like a jewel on a peak and can be seen from a long distance. Freestanding rock surfaces have been used to build monasteries on top of them, one wall at a time, by Buddhist Lamas who live here to learn and meditate. The tough cold climate has not been seized as an excuse to compromise on aesthetics. While the outer walls are usually in white with demarcated windows and ornate doors, the inside walls are covered over by stories of the Buddha and the Bodhisattvas. One wonders what inspired these people to build atop hills, and how they developed their own unique architectural style, using local material like mud blocks and local techniques to build structures without deep foundations.

At the Brihdeeswara Temple in Thanjavur, every guide will tell you about the huge round monolithic stone that adorns the top of the shikhara. It was once covered in gold; and even today, it shimmers when the morning sunrays fall on it. Its delicate balance makes you wonder if the giant temple shikhara sways at times to keep the huge round stone balanced atop it. The story of this huge eighty-ton granite stone getting lifted to a height of more than two hundred feet is one that legends are made of. There are various theories about how the stone was taken up. The most accepted one says that a ramp more than a mile long was built to push the stone up, and elephants were used to pull it up, while men pushed it up from the other end. We do know that ramps were frequently used in temple construction for transporting material, but we really do not know much about the other techniques and technologies used. Is it time for us to do some systematic and structured research to learn more about the engineering methods, formulae and techniques used in the past in India? Is there a possibility that we can use some, or all of them, in modern construction? I can definitely assure you that our modern buildings would look far more aesthetic if we start approaching architecture like our ancestors who built these temples, forts and palaces did, in which meaningful aesthetics dominate and everything else remains quietly hidden.

Vidyashankara Temple at Sringeri

Our ancestors understood well the skies and the movement of celestial bodies too. No wonder, they synchronized most of their buildings, festivals, and everyday life with these movements. At most ancient temples, you discover some alignment of it with the movement of the sun, moon, or other celestial bodies. The summer and winter solstices are the best days to observe this alignment in many temples. One of the best demonstrations of this can be seen at the Vidyashankara Temple located on the banks of Tunga River in Sringeri. While the place is more famous for Sri Sringeri Math and the Sharadamba Temple next door, archaeologically, architecturally, and aesthetically, this temple catches your eyes the most. Not only does this stone temple with an unusual shape look beautiful, it is an ode to the twelve zodiac signs. The temple mandapa stands on twelve pillars, each of which represents the twelve zodiac signs through which the sun passes every year. Four of these pillars are in the corners and are hence bigger, and eight are regular square pillars. As you enter the temple, you encounter the pillar of Aries; if you walk clockwise around the mandapa, past the pillars, and reach the final pillar of Pisces, you will find yourself back at the entrance door. If you know the symbols representing the zodiac signs, it is fun to locate them on the pillars. In some of them, they are easily visible, while in others you have to look intently for them. Now, the engineering wonder here is that the first rays of the morning sun fall on the pillar of the zodiac sign through which the sun is currently transiting. I remember visiting this temple in December when the sun was passing through Sagittarius, and the priest confirmed that the first rays of the morning sun did indeed fall on the Sagittarius pillar during those days. In fact, a small utsav murti had been installed next to this pillar and puja was being performed for it.

Twice a year, the Mahalakshmi Temple in Kolhapur celebrates Kiranotsava for three days. On the first day, the sun's rays fall on Mahalakshmi's feet, on her middle on the second day, and on the third day, they illuminate her entire vigraha. When I saw the pictures of Kiranotsava that literally means 'the festivals of the rays', I was in total awe. If you have visited this temple, you would know that the garbhagriha or the sanctum is far too deep inside the temple for the sun's rays to reach it. But for the electrical lighting, the garbhagriha would be really dark all through the day. This in-built mechanism to ensure that twice a year, precisely for three days, the sun's rays would pay homage to the presiding deity of the temple underlines not just the precise knowledge of the movement of celestial bodies that our ancestors possessed, but also their ability to blend it in their architecture in a way that the celestial bodies that we worship become an integral part of the temple and its annual routine. This temple is not alone, there are many temples wherein the sun's rays touch the deity on the summer and winter solstices alone. We already saw that the Kopeshwar Mahadev Temple at Khidrapur has an open-to-sky swarga mandapa built in alignment with Kartik month's full moon, called Kartik Purnima. I wonder if these principles of building temples in sync with the movement of the sun and the planets have been documented in manuscripts? Have they been studied, or are they still waiting to be unearthed?

At the Jantar Mantar in Jaipur, I spent three hours trying to understand the functioning of the various instruments there. The place is quite intriguing for the uninitiated, with its large triangular walls, huge hanging metallic roundels, red and white scooped out bowls with lines etched all over them, and many curvilinear walls trying to touch the sky. It is a like a geometry box from your school, enlarged manifold and spread out in the open. You know it has something to do with studying the sky but hardly anyone knows just how. You can walk up to the yantras with your sun sign and still not perceive that it can predict your future for you. It takes some patience to convince a guide to explain to you the working of each of these yantras. Most guides will show you how you can read the current time of Jaipur with the two different Samrat Yantras—which are simple, triangular yantras aligned to the axis of Jaipur. The shadows of these walls give you the local time with a precision of up to two seconds. This is the simplest of the instruments at Jantar Mantar. You have to persist and ask your guide to explain to you about all the other instruments there. You will be surprised to see the movement of celestial bodies mapped on earth through these simple looking tools, and that they give you precise readings as well. You can study constellations, the trajectory of the sun through different zodiac constellations, and its path during *dakshinayana* or *uttarayana*. You can also locate your nakshatra on the Raj Yantra that maps all the constellations. The biggest surprise for me was the fact that the Jantar Mantar is still being used to predict monsoons. On the afternoon of the full moon day of the Ashadh month, astrologers come here and use these instruments to learn how good or bad the rains would be in the surrounding desert regions. It heartens me that we still use the tools of our ancestors, and that the knowledge for this is still available with us. I do hope some of us will take it up from where our ancestors left off and build upon their knowledge of astronomy. Other observatories by Sawai Jai Singh exist at Ujjain, Varanasi, Delhi, and Mathura. I hope students in these cities at least understand them enough to explain it to the rest of us.

Coming to metallurgy, the Iron Pillar at the Qutub Complex in Delhi is quite famous for its antiquity, and for the fact that it refuses to rust despite standing in the sun and rain since the fourth century, at the very least. This iron pillar was transported from the Udaygiri Caves near Bhopal in Central India. As a young professional working in Delhi, I often visited it, mostly with the intent to hug the pillar with my arms curling around it backwards and try to get my hands to touch each other. The popular belief is that, if you can achieve this, all your wishes would come true. I do not remember clearly, but it seems to me that I might have just about managed it, for my wishes do come true, but in a form and shape of their own.

Years later, when I moved to Bangalore and trekked to the Kodchadari Hills in the Western Ghats in Karnataka, I would discover the thirty-two feet high cousin of Delhi's Iron Pillar, standing tall in front of the Mookambika Devi Temple. This one too has stayed rust-free for over 2400 years, in an area that gets one of the heaviest rainfalls in the world. The Internet tells me of a third such iron pillar, which is now in fragments, in Dhar near Indore in Madhya Pradesh. We do not even know how many more such pillars and other iron equipment existed. We do see some of them as part of clamps used in some temples or stone structures. They come from the same family of rust-free iron casting.

When you drive from Sibasagar in Assam, from Johat or Guwahati, you encounter a sixty-meter-long monolithic stone bridge on the Namdang River. Our driver stopped just before the bridge to show us this three hundred-year-old stone bridge built by the Ahom kings who ruled from Sibasagar. Cement was yet to take birth then, but rivers had to be crossed. The Namdang Bridge is slightly convex in shape, I assume this is as much a design to manage the flow of water beneath it, as to manage the flow of traffic above it. The sculpted pillars of the bridge remind you that art was always an integral part of the Ahoms' lives; no matter what they created, some art had to adorn it. Whether incorporating artistic or auspicious motifs on built structures of all kinds was a ritual that was followed, or adopted just for its aesthetic value, is anybody's guess. It is said that this stone bridge was built in Bengal and brought here. This tells us a lot about the knowledge and expertise that the people of North East India had in stone-sculpting, bridge engineering and transportation of heavy structures. Remember, it is a land with almost no natural source of stone. On a different note, major temple towns in Bengal like Bankura and Bishnupur have terracotta temples—a lovely innovation in clay in the absence of stone.

Years later, I would hear about the Athara Naal Bridge in the ancient town of Puri, which gets mentioned in folk songs sung by pilgrims approaching the Jagannath temple. This bridge also appears in Pattachitra paintings that depict the journey to Jagannath Puri, of which it is an important landmark. I made a mental note to find this bridge when I visited Puri, though I was not sure if it still existed. As we entered Puri, I saw a lovely bridge on an almost dry Musa River. The bridge looked medieval though it finds a mention in ancient legends about Puri. An IGNCA report confirms that the current bridge was built in the late 18th century, over a pre-existing bridge. Legend says that king Indradyuman—in whose name one of the five tirthas of Puri exist—built this bridge with eighteen corbelled arches by sacrificing his eighteen sons to the river, without which the bridge could not be built. Could this be one of the oldest bridges of India that has been renovated constantly, making it a living piece of heritage? I do not know, but I do know that it is one of those few heritage structures that are still in use, living proudly, and even finds mention in our scriptures.

India's most adorable bridge technology has to be the Living Root Bridges of Meghalaya. What an innovative way to guide the living roots of trees to create a bridge that strengthens as the roots grow. No need to source material, no need to actively maintain it, and no guilt of damaging the environment! The tribal communities who developed these bridges live close to nature and have an intimate relationship with nature, which allows them to play with it for their day-to-day needs. I am keeping my fingers crossed for urbanites to take inspiration and create innovative products that use the philosophy of 'No material sourced from outside'.

Most of our history that we get to read has been written in the last couple of centuries either by curious British officers who would have found our ancient heritage absolutely overwhelming, or a little later by Indians who were trained with the same western view on Indian heritage. The overarching narrative presented of India is that of a spiritual space, which it is, without a doubt. However, for some reason they missed spelling out the outstanding engineering these monuments and public buildings have been built with. I would not blame them, for most of us too have missed it for the longest time. The aesthetic beauty of these structures captures you, regales you in its stories, overwhelms you with its grandeur, and tickles you with its rhythmic symmetry. However, the phenomenal engineering that is the cornerstone of all these structures remains unrecognized. I would go to the extent of saying that the engineering in these structures was so perfect that it remains invisible, letting the other elements and the purpose of the buildings take center stage.

Shilpa shastra texts have remained confined to the small community of sthapatis who continue to use them. Some scholars may have studied them, but these texts are not really available in the public domain. On whatever that is available in the public domain, not many discourses on them have taken place, for us average laypersons to understand them. I trust a couple of new age universities offer courses on the history of engineering sciences in India. Be that as it may, personally, I am looking forward to it being integrated with mainstream engineering and technology courses, so that our young engineers can understand our ancient engineering concepts, and hopefully, take both knowledge and inspiration from them.

Relearning the Language of Time and Space

सहस्रयुगपर्यन्तमहर्यद्ब्रह्मणो विदुः।
रात्रिं युगसहस्रान्तां तेऽहोरात्रविदो जनाः॥

—Bhagavad Gita 8.17

One day of Brahma lasts a thousand cycles of the four ages, and his night too extends for the same span of time. The wise who know this understand the reality about day and night.

I was in Kanchipuram, going from temple to temple, walking through its streets at a time of the year when it is perpetually hot and humid. I had zero knowledge of Tamil and there was not much literature or information available on this temple town in English or Hindi, the two languages that I was conversant with. At the Kanchi Kamakshi Temple, I was pleasantly surprised to see the purohit speak fluent Hindi, as did almost everyone at the Kanchi Kamkoti Peeth. However, aside of these places, the people of the town knew only Tamil, mostly.

In a couple of days, I figured out that the Tamil pronunciation of Sanskrit words is a little different; many a time, "Ga" becomes "Ka", "Sha" becomes "Sa" or "Cha", "Pa" becomes "Ba", and so on and so forth. So, Shiva becomes Siva and Gomati becomes Komati. With this mapping in mind, I could decipher a number of Tamil words, and almost all the nouns. At the smaller temples, when I spoke to the purohits, I spoke slowly and in as much Sanskritized Hindi as possible, and sometimes, just the Sanskrit words spoken in Tamilized form. Lo and behold, I could communicate. I am not saying I could have a free-flowing conversation, but as a traveler, I could gather what I wanted; I could communicate. If a Hindi-speaking North Indian can communicate with Tamil-speaking people, rest assured, you can communicate with anyone in India if you know any one of the Indian languages well. Having said that, you may have to pay a lot of attention to the sound of the local dialect, and make your words sound like it—for instance, in Bengal, I am called "Onuradha." That is all it takes to communicate in Bharat! Having said that, this reference to language is not what this chapter's title is alluding to!

The Girnar inscription of Skandagupta talks about a cloudburst in 456 CE that led to the breach of a lake called Sudarshana, which was probably a lake associated with a dam. The inscription talks about the strength of the lake before it describes the breach, to emphasize the extent of the damage. It tells us the exact date and time of the cloudburst and says that the clouds poured so much rain that the earth became the ocean. It goes on to describe all the things impacted by the cloudburst, from trees to shelters. The inscription says that, with its waters empty, the lake turned ugly, like a sandy desert. The description of this incomplete inscription is poetic even when it talks about the devastation created by the cloudburst. It does not seem to be recording a bare factual statement about a climatic disaster for the meteorological department of its times. The inscription says it all so poetically, even while incorporating all the scientific data and facts needed to be communicated to us, the future generations, about the state of the environment in the region then. If those ancestors were to read our public records today, they would certainly be disappointed.

Ghats of Sarayu in Ayodhya

Kalidasa, in Raghuvamsam, describes the city of Ayodhya while narrating the stories of generations of solar dynasty that ruled from here, and whose genealogy he captures in his magnum opus. He also describes the water sports that happened in the waters of the Sarayu and the multi-storey mansions of Ayodhya, among other things. If you read the Raghuvamsam and then visit Ayodhya, you are bound to be disappointed. Besides the Sarayu, there is nothing there now in this dusty little town of Uttar Pradesh to match Raghuvamsam's beautiful description of Ayodhya. Even if you take into account the fact that the city that Kalidasa talks about must have come from his poetic imagination as much as it would actually have existed on the banks of the Sarayu, his descriptions make you long to go on a pilgrimage to Ayodhya.

However, such linguistic expression par excellence is also not what I wish to talk about in this chapter, though, I do hope that some of us would learn to express facts and thoughts like our ancestors did, and write the 21st century accounts of our towns and cities in such poetic verses.

There is another language that one learns, or rather relearns, when one travels across this country. I do not know if it has a name; hopefully, it will find a new name. It is the language in which our ancestors spoke. No, it is not the language that linguists talk about, or the scripts they identify. It is the language of metaphors that our ancestors used to communicate. It is a language that everyone understood inherently. It is a language that served as a carrier of culture, irrespective of which script it was written in, or even what words were used to speak it. In fact, more often than not, this language does not really need a script to write it down!

Temples on the Ghats of Tapi River in Burhanpur

I was standing on the ghats of the Tapti River in Burhanpur, close to the Madhya Pradesh-Maharashtra border for the evening arti of the river. The steep steps leading down to the river are dotted with small Shiva temples in bright colors, each of them at a different level, and painted in a different color. The photographer in me found it a fascinating frame to capture, but I was to learn that there was more to this interesting juxtaposition of colors on the riverside than what met the eye. Bang in the middle of the river stands a life-size sculpture of an elephant and a baby elephant. When I visited this place, in August, only the orange-colored back of the adult elephant was visible, and I was told that when the water level became low, one could see both the elephants. Watching the river while I waited for the evening arti, I began to realize that the Shiva temples behind me as well as the elephant sculptures in front of my eyes—were actually water markers. The gentleman who single-handedly does the Tapti arti every evening—lighting a lamp, singing the Tapti Mahatmay, and handing over the lamp to a boatman who in turn would leave it in the middle of the river—sat back to chat with me. He told me that all those small Shiva temples were indeed flood markers. He pointed to a temple in bright red color and said, "If the water level touches this temple, this means that there will be floods in Surat the next day." Today, of course, you can just call up and warn the people of Surat, but in the good old days, a messenger had to be sent to warn the people there. This was an awe-inspiring story. I kept looking at the temples and wondered if each of them was associated with the water levels in a distant city or village. How evolved our engineering practices were, and how well woven they were with our cultural ethos. No jarring mechanical equipment was needed, nor special skills, to read the flood situation—one needed to just remember these tales and pass them on to the next generation!

Umananda island is the world's smallest river island. It is actually just a peacock-shaped hill standing in the middle of the Brahmaputra River, so close to Guwahati city that it hardly takes a ten-minute boat ride to reach it. The hill here is called the Bhasmachal Hill, as it is believed that it is here that Kamdeva was turned to ashes or *bhasma* by Shiva.

Remember, the old name of this region is Kamrupa. On top of this hill is the small Umananda Temple dedicated to Shiva and Parvati as Uma, built by the Ahom kings who ruled over Assam for a long time. You could say that the whole of this island is a hill platforming a temple on its top, with some ancient sculptures scattered around. No one lives on this island.

The boatmen told me a folklore about the flooding of the Brahmaputra, which is a devastating one, year after year. This is an accepted way of life on the banks of this river. He said, no matter how bad the floods were, the floodwaters never enter the temple premises, and that the day the floodwaters entered the temple, the city of Guwahati would drown. Now, this was told more as a matter of faith, as a folk tale, that the floodwaters do not dare to enter the home of Umananda. Be that as it may, my interpretation of this is simple: The temple is a water level marker. If the water in the river is about to touch the doors of the temple, it is time to evacuate the city of Guwahati and move away from the river.

There is a language hidden in our architecture and sculptures, and this is true not just in the case of our majestic stone temples—which, as we now understand—are telling us stories from our ancient historical past. It is inbuilt in all our creations. Nothing, it seems, was without meaning, even when it looks merely aesthetic at first glance.

In his landmark book '*Aaj bhi kahre hain talab*', Anupam Mishra talks about the water bodies of India—meticulously documenting communities who built all kinds of lakes, ponds and stepwells, and the methods, techniques and folklore associated with the water bodies. In his book, he mentions pillars erected next to certain ponds, especially in dry regions like Rajasthan. Sometimes, instead of a pillar, there is a small temple with the image of a deity. He gives an example of how people spoke about the water levels and what it meant for the community. Let us say one of the pillars has a standing image of Krishna playing his flute. When the water level touches the feet of Krishna, the message that goes across the villages it supports is that there is just enough water to last the whole year; that you may not have water to splurge, but if you use water wisely, it will last the whole year. If the water reaches the navel of Krishna, there is good amount of water, and some splurging can be afforded. If the water level reaches the flute, it is an early warning sign, no more water can be accommodated. If the water level crosses Krishna's head—it means disaster. When I was reading this part, it reminded me of an oft-used phrase in Hindi "*Pani sir se nikal gaya hai*" for situations that are totally out of your control and have caused irreversible damage. It made me understand the reference point of this phrase. It arose from the grave scenario forecast when the water level goes above the head of the marker deity, indicating an emergency that is beyond anyone's control. I infer it may have called for vacating places close to the water bodies.

This opened a whole new dictionary for me to study. I wondered what the stepwells, which are full of ornate structures all over their walls, are trying to tell us. I was reminded of the Sheshashayee Vishnu often seen at the base of stepwells, indicating that the people using these stepwells treated it as their own Ksheersagar—the ocean of milk. This may have also served to ensure that the stepwell was kept clean, for who would dare dirty the ocean where Vishnu sleeps peacefully.

This prompts me to question: Do we need to look at ornate sculptures beyond just their iconography and the stories they present. Is there a hidden chronicle that we are yet to decipher? Do they carry ecological warnings that we have not yet learned to interpret? Are there mathematical equations within them that we have not yet solved?

Once, we were visiting South Sikkim and North Bengal. In the Dooars region of Bengal, the narrow strip of land connecting North East India to the rest of India and sandwiched between Bhutan and Bangladesh, lies the elephant corridor. This is an area ruled by elephants. At Siliguri, we were staying in an army area with our family friends who had been posted there then. On an early morning walk, we saw an intriguing board that said: '*Maharaj ke aane par aur aag lagne par soochit karen*' meaning 'Please inform if the Maharaj comes or if there is a fire'; this was followed by emergency phone numbers to be dialed. This board left us wondering who this Maharaj was. We went back home and asked our hosts about this and they had a hearty laugh before sharing that this was how elephants were called there. Yes, "Maharaj ji" means elephants. Our hosts then regaled us with various elephant stories, including some where they had had to vacate the house or stay locked inside the house, as Maharaj ji with his/her extended families were strolling outside, enjoying their walks, and would play around with anything that came in their way. These stories sound hilarious in retrospect, but in reality, it can be scary, if and when herds of elephants go on a rampage.

We spent a couple of days in the Jaldapara National Park and its Hollong Range, where you get to see large groups of elephants, single-horned rhinoceros, and thousands of bright and colorful yellow-footed green pigeons. On an elephant safari through wild grass as tall as the elephant itself, I heard more stories about elephant herds. Here, the mahout kept using the word "*Mahakal*" for elephants on a rampage. I asked him if they were not called "Maharaj". He said, "Usually, they *are* Maharaj, when they are in their peaceful mode, but when they go on a rampage destroying everything in sight, including small homes and fields, we say '*Mahakal aaye hain*' (Mahakal has come)." Mahakal, as we know, is one of the names of Shiva, both as the 'Deity of Time' and as the 'Deity of Death'. So, elephants here are seen as emperors who sometimes come in the form of death. No one ever calls them *haathi* or elephants here, barring a few ignorant tourists like us.

What a lovely use of language to acknowledge that elephants are the rulers of this land. We may live here only if they are happy, only if we live in harmony with them. Even when they destroy our homes or our crops, we do not curse them; we see them as Mahakal—the deity who has to destroy, so that new creation can happen. Isn't this a language that most of us are ignorant of, a language that never lets you forget who the supreme being on this land is? We do get to hear of incidents of destruction by elephants, even so, no one calls for killing the elephants or hurting them. We just accept what they do, since we accept that their right on the land is as much as ours.

In the narrow lanes of Vrindavan leading to the famous Banke Bihari Temple, where piles of *pedas* and rows of *kachoriwalas* tempt you, I was standing in a narrow shop, eating my pani puri. Suddenly, someone holding a heavy basket, whose path I was blocking said, "Radhe, *hatiye na,*" asking me to make way. Since 'Radha' is a part of my name, my first instinct was—how does he know my name? Then it struck me that this is Vrindavan, where every interaction begins and ends with 'Radhe Radhe'. From hello to goodbye to excuse me, everything is communicated by 'Radhe Radhe' here. Still, it was new to me that every woman on the street gets addressed as Radhe here. Later, I would come to observe many such instances of women, from young girls to old women, all being called Radhe. Radha is not just a deity here; she becomes a living embodiment in every woman in her kshetra. I loved the sound of it. I felt I became a part of Braj by being called Radha. I realized that languages like this have the power to make us feel welcome and accepted in the land we are visiting, while also introducing us to its ethos. I should not forget to mention that I made way for the person with the heavy basket with a broad smile on my face.

Currently, I am trying to read a few Indian scriptures first-hand, in the original. So far, I have only read Goswami Tulsidas's Ramcharitmanas, the Durga Saptashati, Devi Bhagwat Puran, Kalidasa's Raghuvamsam and some sections of the Skand Puran and Padma Puran relevant to travels across ancient cities of India. I have a long list of scriptures that I want to read after this. Reading these scriptures has taken me to another world. While growing up, my mental makeup was that these books would be filled with *karma kand* or ritualistic details and mandate following them on a daily basis, and that the scriptures would discuss nothing beyond worshipping of the millions of deities we have. I could not have been more wrong. As I read, I am discovering that every possible subject on earth is embedded in them. The stories in these scriptures beautifully blend and fuse into what we would slot under various heads today—including science, technology, astronomy, law, psychology, aesthetics, storytelling, communications, political science, economics, ethics, and what not.

While reading the Ramcharitmanas, the biggest impression that I took away was the description of Ram Rajya. Ram Rajya is a term we often hear, sometimes even in a satirical tone. I used to think that Ram Rajya was something that happened automatically as soon as Sri Ram sat on the throne of Ayodhya. He probably waved a magic wand and Ram Rajya just descended. I can only laugh at my naivety now. Goswami Tulsidas tells us with minute details what Ram Rajya actually means. He talks less about how Sri Ram ruled, and more about how people behaved in his reign. He explains how society stays in balance when everyone behaves and works as per the dharma of their *varna* and *ashram*. This essentially means acting as required by your age and stage in life. Tulsidas goes on to define the environment during Ram Rajya—trees bore the best fruits; the wind was always mild, fragrant and cool; the river water was clean and so were her banks; the animals roamed around freely without hurting anyone. The Ramcharitmanas talks about economics too, saying that the markets were lined with the best products, and the businessmen sitting in their shops looked like Kuber—the deity of wealth, sitting on his riches. It describes the prosperity of Ayodhya through a lovely description of the opulent houses and palaces, while not forgetting to mention the renunciate yogis coexisting in the same city on the banks of the Sarayu River. It is such a beautiful description. To begin with, it sounds utopian, but when you ponder on it a little, you know that this is exactly what we need to do as a society to usher in Ram Rajya. The king or the leader has to lead by example, and the people have to follow his example. The king alone cannot do much. We will have Ram Rajya when each one of us does what we are supposed to do in the best possible manner. It is not a one-way street, and it is not limited to one entity in the society being happy.

There are other sections in Ramcharitmanas that talk about philosophy, human behavior, and about the rights and duties of human beings. All this comes wrapped in the veneer of a story that we all know, and so, when we read these scriptures, we are not wondering what would happen next in the story; we already know it. We know that Ram, Lakshman and Sita would go to the forest, that Sita will get abducted, and that they will return to Ayodhya. So, we focus on the mental make-up of the characters and the dialogues between them. We understand their dilemmas and learn the driving principles they employ to take decisions. They resonate with our own dilemmas, and this is where these scriptures can guide us.

Kevat *samvad* is the famous dialogue between Sri Ram and Kevat—the boatman on whose boat Ram, Sita and Lakshman crossed the Ganga on their way to the forest. After the trio gets down on the other side and Sri Ram tries to pay Kevat, Kevat says he cannot take Ram's *utraai*. Utraai refers to the fee for getting down from the boat. Now, compare this to today's scenario, with regard to tickets we buy for boat rides or for any such service. Most of the time, we pay before we board the boat. The service provider charges you to board the boat or for the ride and not really to take you to your destination. In contrast, in the days of Sri Ram, as Tulsidas communicates without using as many words, the fee was paid after the traveler reached his destination, when he had been helped to reach his goal, and not for the ride, and not if he hadn't been taken to the other bank for some reason. Indeed, language chronicles the threads of culture in invisible ways, the reason why many translations miss capturing these nuances.

A text like Kalidasa's Raghuvamsam takes you through the entire geography of India when he describes each of the suitors present at the swayamvara of a princess. I have noticed this repeatedly across scriptures, that through them, the reader gets to learn the precise political geography of India at those points in time. Authors of these scriptures walk the reader along with their protagonists, who might be the girl for whom the swayamvar was conducted, or the one who would eventually win her. This is because, as the girl walks past the suitors, each suitor is described to her in terms of which kingdom he came from, what his kingdom is known for, and of course the personal traits of the man—as a kind of primer that would allow the girl to make an informed choice. Although I doubt the girls of those times were ignorant and made their decisions on the spur of the moment, driven by factors like good looks alone. Reading these descriptions, we virtually take a tour of India through her kingdoms and their landscapes, their produce, their rivers, and every other noticeable feature.

Time and Our Perceptions of It

Time is a flexible concept in India. At one end, we calculate *muhurat*—the precise auspicious time to commence any new initiative in life; at the other end, we hardly reach anywhere on time. For a traveler, it demands flexibility at another level. Our language and concept of time and space can be as absolute as they are relative. When it comes to calculations, it looks like our ancestors could be far more precise than what our modern-day calibrations allow. When describing time in day-to-day language, the scales they used could be as random as they wished; it was somewhat of a poetic license that they took, even when language constructs were recognized.

In our scriptures, units of time are defined in terms of the length of a day of Brahma and the divisions there of. At the lower end of the scale, the minutest division of time goes right down to the time taken to blink an eye. Let us get a sense of this scale:

1 *Mahakalpa* = 100 Years of Brahma

1 Year of Brahma = 360 Day/Night cycles

1 Day of Brahma = 1 Kalpa

1 Kalpa = 432,00,00,000 Human Years

1 Kalpa = 14 Manvantar

1 Manvantar = 71 Chaturyuga

1 Chaturyuga = 1 Satyuga/Kritayuga + 1 Tretayuga + 1 Dwaparyuga + 1 Kaliyuga

1 Satyuga = 17,28,000 Years

1 Tretayuga = 12,96,000 Years

1 Dwaparyuga = 8,64,000 Years

1 Kaliyuga = 4,32,000 Years

Each Manvantar has a presiding Manu.

Now, if this sounds mind boggling to you, you are not alone. I got a better sense of it when I tried to place myself on this time scale. If you have participated in Hindu rituals, you might have noticed that the purohits conducting it actually zoom in on a point in space-time as defined below, to indicate the time, place and purpose of the puja.

So then, now, we are in:

In terms of Brahma's life, we are in the first day of the fifty-first year of his life. It is also called the Shwet-Varaha kalpa.

Of the fourteen manvantars within the Shwet-Varaha kalpa, we are in the seventh manvantar, with Vaivasvata Muni as the current Manu, so this manvantar is called Vaivasvat manvantar.

Within the seventh manvantar, we are in the twenty-eighth cycle of chaturyuga.

Of the four yugas in the twenty-eighth cycle of the seventh manvantar, we are in kaliyuga, which started after the Mahabharata war, which in turn marked the end of the current cycle of dwaparyuga. This means we are pretty much at the beginning of the kaliyuga.

Do you get a sense of the momentary nature of our lives when you look at this time scale?

Now, let us change the lens and zoom in to understand the other end of this time scale. I am sure you would have heard the phrase "*Mahurat nikla ja raha hai*" or "*Abhi muhurat nahi nikla*"—commonly used phrases to convey "The right time is slipping by" and "The right time has not yet come" respectively. Muhurats gets printed on wedding invitations. I always looked upon the muhurat time as the auspicious time calculated for the event. It took me a long time to understand that the muhurat is actually a unit of time that equals forty-eight minutes. This means that thirty muhurats constitute the twenty-four hours of a day.

The muhurat is one of the most practical units of time, used by us even today in everyday life. For example, when you are told to get up at Brahma muhurat, it simply means getting up two muhurats or one hour and thirty six minutes before your local sunrise time.

At the other end of the scale, there are other units of time that go to such minuscule levels that they are as difficult to comprehend as are the days and years of Brahma.

One muhurat is equal to two ghatis or ghadis. Now, this instantly lets me make sense of phrases like "*do ghadi*" or "*ghadi bhar*", knowing ghadi to be essentially twenty-four minutes. One ghadi is thirty-one *pala,* that means a pala is roughly forty-six seconds, and knowing it, I now get a sense of what a '*pala*', which is mentioned in so many Hindi songs, means. If you keep on dividing this unit of time, you will arrive at *paramanu* which is a rather incomprehensible measure of 10^{-7} seconds.

I had to read both ends of the timeline many times, and in many different contexts to internalize them, and I am still not sure how well I understand them. I do understand that what we comprehend is just a small part of a long continuum that we really cannot comprehend. To understand better, I need to learn and use the language used in ancient India more often.

Coming back to my travels, having studied some scholarly works on Indian heritage, I started looking for dates and times concerning the places I visited. I started asking around for the oldest structural remains of the places I visited, and the dates of construction of the structures that were still to be seen around. I always got some vague answers, such as—it is old, very old, or *baap-dada ke samay ka hai* (it belongs to the time of our ancestors). When they did quote a date, I got as many different dates as the number of people I asked.

When we talk about the past, we have a really fluid sense of time. We are not really bothered about how distant the past is. It really does not matter whether Sri Ram and Sri Krishna lived five hundred years or five thousand years or fifty thousand years ago. We just know that they lived, and what matters is what their lives taught us. Our sense of time is as vague for events and happenings, as it is precise when it comes to calculations. I remember, at a small temple in Puri, the signboards were in Odia, a language I cannot read. When I asked a fellow pilgrim who spoke Odia to read it out for me, he gave me a strange look. He said: How does it matter what is written? Go, pray to Jagannath, take his blessings, nothing else matters. This kind of summed up how, when not engaged in doing precise calculations, we relate to the past, present and the future.

Defining Sacred Spaces

The concept of space is as knotted as that of time. However, I discovered it in a different fashion during my travels, from the way artists used the space available to them for storytelling. Our ancient storytellers rarely told stories in a linear fashion; they had their own convoluted ways of telling the stories. Sometimes, they virtually recreated the stories for you, somewhat like creating a make-believe film set to tell the story; and sometimes, they just said a part of the story and left the rest for you to read, listen or recall.

I was at the Ajanta Caves' Cave No. 1, known for its exquisite paintings of Bodhisattva Padmapani and Bodhisattva Vajrapani. While the two paintings captivate you with their fine details and their peaceful stance, you tend to get lost in the multiple scenes painted on the walls of the dark caves. The first question that intrigues you while your eyes are still adjusting to the interiors of this cave that is dark even during the day is: How did the artists paint such intricate details inside these dark caves? Once your eyes adjust to the darkness, you see a mélange of scenes running into each other. The guides quickly tell you a story or two. They usually have their favorite scenes to show—the ones that have the maximum surprise element like the presence of Persian merchants on the walls. It took me a couple of visits, some reading, and a course by Dr. Vidya Dehejia to understand the way stories flow in ancient Indian Art. My biggest learning was that familiarity of the viewer with the story is assumed by the artist. The purpose of the paintings, as our ancestors saw it, was for them to serve as reminders of the messages they wished to convey or the rituals that you should not forget while you are there.

Jataka Tales narrate the stories of Bodhisattvas, the ones who are on the path to become a Buddha but are not yet there. These tales are the most common theme in Buddhist art, along with the life of Sakyamuni Buddha—be it sculptures or paintings. You find sculptures all around Buddhist stupas like the Sanchi Stupa, and in caves like Ajanta, Ellora, and Bagh. So, a story may be told using a single scene from the story. For example, at the Undavalli Caves near Vijayawada in Andhra Pradesh, there is a single scene depicting Hanuman and Sita in Ashok Vatika at Lanka, and this sums up the entire Ramayana for you. There are other sculptures telling other stories, but this is the only scene that represents the Ramayana in this cave. I saw the same scene used to depict the Ramayana at the Kopeshwar Mahadev Temple near Kolhapur in Maharashtra, although the temple walls inside and outside are lined with all kinds of sculptures. The scene chosen may be the key action point in the story, or the final outcome of the story—the idea is to convey the values of the story.

At times, there is a linear or sequential telling of the story wherein scenes from the story are depicted one after the other in the order they happen in the story. I recall only two instances of this—one is at the Parambanan Temple in Yogyakarta in Indonesia where the whole of the Ramayana is depicted in a series of panels, which you can see as you do the parikrama of the temple. This feels like watching a Ramayana performance as you walk around. As for the second instance, there are two large stone panels in Ellora's Kailashnath Temple or Cave No. 16, where the Ramayana and the Mahabharata are depicted in a linear fashion on a single stone. Viewing this feels like reading a visual version of the epics, quite like modern-day comic strips.

On a related note, at the Sanchi Stupa, on one of the *torans*, the scene of Buddha's leaving home is depicted without really picturing Buddha. It shows Buddha's departure from home by showing a horse going out of the palace with a parasol on it, and the horse returning to the palace without the parasol, indicating that Buddha stepped out of the palace but never returned. In early Buddhist art, Buddha is depicted using his icons like the parasol, lion, or lotus, and not with his own image. The Buddha images that we see in museums and Buddhists sites came a little later. There are a couple of other styles where multiple scenes are shown in a single frame, and you have to know the story to figure out the sequence.

At the other end of the spectrum of storytelling in India, in some places, you can see a clear demarcation between the sculpted panels, as in the carvings of Rani ki Vav in Patan. The figures of Madanikas or Sur Sundaris—beautiful women in happy poses, or couples in love are used to punctuate these narratives. Juxtaposing such images to demarcate the spiritual scenes is puzzling, and this is a puzzle that, to the best of my knowledge, is yet to be solved.

The most elaborate and complicated storytelling happens in a narrative network mode, wherein artists recreate the places figuring in the story. Say, if Ramayana is to be depicted, one part of the wall would be Ayodhya, another would be Lanka, and yet another may be Panchvati, or forests in general. In this story-telling approach, the scenes are depicted in the respective places where they happened, in the spaces earmarked on the wall. So, the space showing Ayodhya would show Dashrath yagna, birth of Ram and his brothers, the brothers coming back with their brides (remember, the wedding happened in Janakpur), Ram leaving for his exile and returning to be a king, and so on. This is the narrative style used to depict many long Jataka tales in the Ajanta Caves. When you stand before these walls, you have the entire universe of the story in front of you and your eyes follow the flow of the story on the cave walls. If the story runs back and forth between two places, so does your gaze.

This re-creation of the story's universe happens not just on walls, but on the ground too, with the stories getting performed. A great example of this is the famous Ramlila of Ramnagar located on the opposite banks of the Ganga, across the city of Varanasi. I am yet to see Ramnagar's Ramlila performance, but I have read the book, 'Actors, Pilgrims, Kings and Gods—The Ramlila of Ramnagar' by my namesake, Anuradha Kapur, who has documented the whole of Ramlila in this book. I picked up this book when I saw the lovely Ramlila masks at Bharat Kala Bhavan Museum at Banaras Hindu University in Varanasi. Soon after, I heard the stories of the same Ramlila at Jnanpravah Museum, where I learnt about Bharat Milap being the world's shortest drama, as on this day, only one scene is enacted with Ram and Bharat coming towards each other from opposite ends and embracing each other.

The entire town of Ramnagar turns into a live stage for the thirty days of the year when Ramlila gets performed here. Different spaces of the village are assigned the roles of the different places figuring in the Ramayana. When the story moves to, say, Lanka, all the villagers walk to the place in the village representing Lanka, and the relevant scene is performed there. The audience is there not just to witness the performance, they are active participants too. They are never the outsiders; they are always part of the scene. Many of them play the smaller roles. At times, when parallel scenes are happening, the audience has to choose which one to be part of. Actors, usually children, playing Ram, Sita and Lakshman are treated just like the deities they essay. They are not allowed to put their feet on the ground. People lift them on their shoulders when they have to move from one place to another. And did you know, even today, in independent India, the Kashi Naresh, the chief patron of the Ramlila and the *yajman* for all the rituals associated with it, plays himself. This is how spaces and roles transform temporarily in this town.

Travel down south to some small villages of Tamil Nadu, not too far from Chennai, and you will find Mahabharata performed in a very similar way here. It is sung, it is told, and it is performed along with the rituals that run almost throughout the day, for as many as twenty to thirty days, with all the villagers participating in the rituals. This performance is called Mahabharata Koothu. In this performance, Dharamraja or Yudhishtra stays inside his temple in the village, as he should not see kaliyuga, but Draupadi comes out to witness and to listen to her own story. The whole village participates in the ritual performances, even though only the lead actors may wear the elaborate masks and costumes. The venue, people and the actors move as the story moves. When the koothu highlights the exile of the Pandavas, the whole village goes on an exile as part of this performance. When Duryodhana is to be killed on the penultimate day called *pandugalam*, there is an actor playing the part of Duryodhana and also a giant mud sculpture of Duryodhana on the ground. The actor performs and fights, but the final blow that kills Duryodhana is directed at the sculpture. The story changes every year as a different group of koothu artists perform. People from places afar come over to witness the performance and they are all treated as the guests of the host village. They say the koothu is another way of preserving memories of past wars, going all the way back to the mega Mahabharata war. What fascinates me about the koothu is how the space is transformed to re-create an all-encompassing story, a story that is told year after year, a story that is known by heart by everyone participating and witnessing it. Some scholars interpret the koothu as a reliving of the epics on the inside and the outside, forging a way to deal with battles inside and outside.

Parikrama – Encircling the Sacred Space

Parikramas or *pradakshina* of a sacred space is a common form of pilgrimage in ancient cultures around the world. In a parikrama, you go around the sacred space in a clockwise circle with the sacred space always on your right and end the journey where you began. It is a process that allows you to take the collective sacred energy from the holy place and recharge yourself. All temples have a pradakshina path or a circumambulatory path going around the garbhagriha. Sometimes, these paths go around not just the presiding deity, but also around all the other deities in the temple. There are also parikramas around sacred water bodies like the Mansarovar Lake, or rivers like the Narmada.

Parikramas happen at various levels. Most pilgrimages would involve some kind of circumambulation around a sacred space. One big parikrama that I did was the Panch Kroshi yatra at Kashi. It is a seventy-five-kilometer path that starts from the Manikarnika Ghat, moves southward on boat towards the Assi Ghat, and then goes around the Kashi Khand after crossing the Assi River, and then the Varuna River, before reaching the northern end of the ghats of the Ganga, from where you again take the boat back to the Manikarnika Ghat to complete your journey. Doing this parikrama, you can see all the ghats from the river; you also see hundreds or maybe thousands of small temples, all on your right-hand side. I was told that all the *dharamshalas* and restrooms come up on your left, and all the temples on your right. There are five *padavs* or stops with slightly bigger temples and much bigger temple tanks. These stops have dharamshalas and other facilities for pilgrims to stay. You stop here to take rest, to listen to the stories, and to connect with the divine. The first padav is at the Kardameshwar Temple, the oldest surviving temple in Kashi. The second one is Bhima Chandi that gets its name from the Devi temple here. The third padav is Rameshwaram that is believed to be built by Sri Ram himself and has temples built by all the four brothers. The fourth padav has five Shivalingas established by the five Pandavas and has murtis commemorating them. The final padav is at the Kapildhara Temple related to Kapil Muni. It took me a whole day to do the yatra, and I was awestruck by the number of small temples I saw on the way. I was pleasantly surprised by the well-maintained roads and apt road signs all along the path. Back home, when I was writing about this for my blog and going through all the images I had taken, I realized that the Panch Kroshi yatra takes you through a Shiva Temple, a Devi Temple, and past footprints of the Ramayana and the Mahabharata before winding up at the temple of Kapil Muni—effectively, this yatra encompasses all the elements of Sanatana Dharma. Kashi has five such parikrama paths, all of them begin and end in and around the Manikarnika Kund, which is believed to be older than the river Ganga. Together, they cover the sacred geography of the oldest and holiest city of India.

A couple of years later, I would do the 14 Kosi yatra of Ayodhya, and this would take me through all the key places associated with not just the Ramayana, but the entire Ikshvaku *vamsha* or the solar dynasty that ruled from Ayodhya. It takes you to the kuti where Bharat lived for fourteen years. You get to see the Sun Temple and a Suraj Kund that is the family deity of the Suryavanshis. You see the Dashrath Samadhi Sthal and many other ancient temples. Ayodhya has three such parikrama paths—5 Kosi, 14 Kosi and 84 Kosi. At Ayodhya, you can start your parikrama anywhere and it is complete when you are back where you started. I remember, I started from a Hanumangarhi temple on one side of the main road. On our way back, I tried getting down at a spot across the road from this temple, but my driver insisted that we cross the road and touch the temple again so that the parikrama is complete. I complied.

A few months later, I did the Govardhan Parikrama in Braj Bhumi. Until I reached there, I only knew that one could walk the entire parikrama path or use a vehicle to go around the sacred hill that Krishna once lifted on his little finger. Once at Govardhan, I was told that one could do a Dandwat Parikrama too, wherein you cover the whole path with your full body. This is how a Dandwat Parikrama is done—you lie on the path face down with your hands stretched and mark the point where your hands reach. You then get up, and walk to the point you marked, and lie down again with your feet at the marked spot, repeating the sequence until the entire twenty-one kilometers are covered! Some couples do it together, taking turns in lying down; this reduces the effort by half, but it is still an arduous journey to take.

108 Dandwat Govardhan Parikrama

Some people walk with a pot of milk that has a small hole in it—it is called the Doodhari Parikrama. Effectively, here, you are marking the path with a trail of milk. It is not unusual to see a thin line of milk on the path you are walking. Most people I saw doing this parikrama were doing it on electric rickshaws, holding out the pot of milk over the road. The most interesting parikrama I discovered was the Sohni Parikrama that is done with a broom in the hand to clean the path as you walk. What a lovely way to make sure the path is kept clean by the very pilgrims who use it. Hardest of these parikramas though is the 108 Dandvat Parikrama, where the pilgrim does 108 rounds of getting up and touching the ground at each spot before moving forward. They use a pile of stones to count the number of rounds. This parikrama takes years to do. At best, a person can cover five–ten meters in a day. On the path, you see many such piles of stones, along with small make-shift temples. These pilgrims, mostly sadhus, spend their lives doing this parikrama. You have to see them to believe their dedication and commitment. Just watching them gives you a sense of reverence for them. Observing their strenuous effort, you also get triggered to realize what may be lacking in your efforts, if you are not getting the desired results of your acts.

It is said that, in the past, you could see the flag of the Puri Jagannath temple when you enter the radius of the Panch Kos, which is an indication that you are in the Puri kshetra, the sacred space of Jagannath. At Maheshwar, at the Narmada Temple on the ghats of the Narmada, I met these frail looking women who were on their Narmada Parikrama and I count them as some of the strongest women I have ever met. They were walking draped in their simple cotton saris, carrying almost nothing with them, staying at temples and ashrams on the way—all along the 2600-kilometer circumference of the Narmada. They were circling the scared geography of the oldest known and one of the most sacred rivers in India.

Every sacred mountain, like the Arunachalam in Tamil Nadu or the Kinner Kailash—the winter home of Shiva in Himachal, has a pilgrimage path going around it. Then, there are pilgrimages like the Vari yatra to Pandharpur wherein everyone walks to the temple. For some of these sacred journeys, there is a designated time of the year, while others can be undertaken at any point in time. Scholars cite many reasons for these pilgrimage paths. To me, they are paths demarcating the sacred spaces from the area around them. A counter argument to this could be: Aren't all spaces sacred? To an extent yes, they are. However, there are certain high energy points on earth, that are further strengthened by the collective spiritual energy of the devotees visiting and meditating there, repeatedly, year after year.

Would we be able to relearn the language of our land and read all that was written by our ancestors in various forms and shapes—in architecture, in sculpture, in engineering, in the cultural nuances of communication, in rituals that took us inward while we performed them outwardly, in wall murals, in scriptures, and in just about everything that has been passed on to us from them? Would this language enrich our life and help us unleash our creativity the way it did for our ancestors?

What is my Dharma?

स्य मुखमासीद् बाहू राजन्यः कृतः।
ऊरू तदस्य यद्वैश्यः पद्भ्यां शूद्रो अजायत॥

—Purush Sukta, Rig Veda 10.90

Brahmins are his mouth, kshatriyas his arms, vaishyas his thighs, and shudras his feet.

Some of the questions that I often face go like this: Which are the temples that I should visit? What are the temples that I should visit in location 'X', if I have limited time there? What is my dharma as an ordinary human being?

After traveling to so many temples and reading—in bits and pieces, in different scriptures—about our ancient history, making a choice can get overwhelming. The fact is, every temple's, and every tirtha's, legend tells us that unless we visit and worship there, our life goals are not achieved. However, one cannot visit all the temples in India. It is just not possible. Even though my primary goal in life is traveling, I know that I cannot possibly travel to even a small percentage of the temples I know of. Every scripture has a list of sacred tirthas to visit and so many dos and don'ts for its followers.

I too had questions, of the kind raised above, once. It took me a lot of time to process all the information that I was consuming to reach this conclusion—you cannot possibly follow all that you are told or all that you read. So then, what is one supposed to do if one wishes to follow dharma? How do you zero in on the places to visit or the system to follow, to lead a contented life? What is my prioritized list of temples and tirthas to visit?

I am not a spiritual guru. I do not even have a formal guru guiding me on this path. The following is what I have gathered from my experiences and have figured out for myself, and it did help me find answers for many of the questions raised above. The answer lies in the simple and rather well-known matrix of varna, ashram and *purushartha*. Like everything else, you can have multiple interpretations of these concepts, depending on who is interpreting these concepts, and even, *when* one is considering the same. This is not a fixed matrix; it is as fluid as life itself. It will keep evolving as you move on in life, as you transit from one stage to another, as your purpose in life moves higher, and as you attain goals and define new goals for yourself. When you are in a dilemma, when you need to decide what you should do and what you should potentially let go of, this matrix does help you decide. It gently guides you towards your dharma, based on these three primary parameters of life.

Matrix of Ashram, Varna & Purushartha

This is the matrix of ashram, varna and purushartha as I understand it.

What is my ashram?

Let us understand the first of these three parameters—ashram. I am sure you have heard of these four stages—*brahmacharya, grihastha, vanaprastha and sanyasa*. These four ashrams span the whole human life, from birth to death. Your life is roughly divided into these four stages, most of the time, sequentially. The number of years spent in each of these stages may vary a little for each one of us, but as average human beings—who go to school, work, retire and leave the body—we all go through these four stages in some fashion. Let us have a brief look at what each of these stages in life mean and what is expected of us during these stages.

Brahmacharya is your childhood and your student life. This is the time you spend with your parents first, and thereafter with your teachers, who prepare you for later life. Who your teachers are depends on what you have chosen to be in life. At this stage, your sole responsibility is to be as good a student as possible and learn as much as possible. Learning could be in any form—such as from books if you are planning to be a teacher, from training and practice if you want to be a professional athlete or performing artist, or by hands-on coding if you want to be a software professional. It is recommended that while you are studying, you direct your entire focus on learning, that everything else takes a backseat. This stage also requires you to follow strict rules so as to lay a strong foundation for good health, to practice good conduct, and to keep away from any distractions. You learn these rules from your parents and teachers, who in turn have learnt it from their experience of life. Having passed through this stage, they are now in a position to teach you.

The second ashram is the grihastha ashram—the time to be a householder. It is the stage that immediately follows the brahmacharya ashram or student life. This is the time to work, earn your living, get married and raise a family. This is the time to take on responsibilities both on the professional front and the home front. On the professional front, you start working to earn your living and to reach your professional goals, whatever they are. On the home front, you get married and lead a householder's life; you give birth to children, raise them, and take care of them. As you move within this grihastha ashram, your children grow and begin to need you less and less, while your parents grow older and start needing you more and more. Both are your responsibility. You, along with your life partner, shoulder the responsibilities of the family as well as your respective careers during this stage. This is the most active stage of your life, as this is when you do most of what you want to do in life. It is that time of your life when you are young, healthy, energetic, and in the working group. It is also the stage when people around you in the other three stages of life are dependent on you—be it your children in brahmacharya ashram, your parents in vanaprastha ashram, or your grandparents in sanyasa ashram. Professionally too, this is the stage when you do most of your life's work as you move up in your career or business. This is also the time to enjoy your life as much as possible.

Vanaprashtha ashram is when you are still active, and your next generation has entered the grihastha ashram and is taking the baton of responsibility from you. You have not yet retired, but retirement is in sight. You probably have started feeling a bit tired of your professional life or may be facing what is now called the mid-career crisis. You have reached an age when niggling health issues might start troubling you, your energy levels start falling a bit. Women start approaching menopause and face issues associated with it. This is the time when you gently hand over your responsibilities to the next generation—both at home and at the workplace. At work, you are approaching the peak of your career. This is the time to focus on building the next generation leadership and teams that can take over from you in a few years' time. This is the time to be a leader who guides and mentors the next generation. You do not really give up your home or your career yet, but you ensure a smooth transition by preparing to hand over, or hand-hold as you hand over the baton, ensure a smooth transition, and assure the next generation that you are at hand to handle difficult situations and help them make crucial decisions.

Sanyasa ashram is the last stage, where you disengage with the world and focus on your inner divinity like a renunciate. By this stage, you have completely handed over all your responsibilities and made yourself redundant for all practical purposes. This is the time when your body ages, but your heart and mind return to a childlike stage. You feel the need to connect with your inner self. You have seen the world and lived your life and you probably realize the futility of it all. Most people tend to spontaneously move towards spiritual pursuits in this stage. No wonder, you see so many retired persons at pilgrimage places and in religious gatherings, though of course, you could say that they are the ones who have time for these pursuits. It is the time to do the yatras or pilgrimages—traveling not just to places, but also into oneself. Having lived a long life, you probably now understand and appreciate what the scriptures are communicating. This is also the time to engage with the generation of your grandchildren. They are not your responsibility, but you are their storytellers, their moral compass, and at times, even their secret keepers. This is the time to do whatever you want to do before the time comes to leave this body and move on. This is the time when you really have nothing to lose, people generally respect you for your age and listen to you.

At a personal level, most of us progress along this trajectory naturally, and make the appropriate adjustments, with slight deviations here and there. As professionals though, it would help if we can identify our transition points and change our work and leadership styles according to our stage in life. For instance, a sanyasi in professional life can be more effective in mentoring than in executing or competing, wherein you guide, but stay outside the system, with no responsibilities.

Now, this is a natural flow in life which we inadvertently follow, even if we are not consciously aware of it. As with every rule, there are exceptions to this flow. Some people may jump from the brahmacharya ashram to the sanyasa ashram if they happen to be dispassionate about worldly life and are keen to pursue their spiritual goals. If you do not have children, you may move directly from the grihastha ashram to the sanyasa ashram. If you are in a creative field, you may remain active longer than others in non-creative careers. Writers do not really retire but what they write may reflect the stage of their life. Just being conscious of your ashram in life can help you sort out many confusions.

What is my varna?

Varna is what defines your primary activities in life, it refers more to a person's professional life, rather than his or her personal life, unlike the ashrams. It is a broad categorization at a societal level, with the activities divided among people in a way that we are interdependent on each other while being experts at what we do. The four broad classifications are—brahmin, kshatriya, vaishya and shudra. You could also call them teachers, warriors, traders, and artisans. This categorization is probably the most misunderstood concept about India. Varna is not a casteist system as has been assumed for many centuries now. In the good old days, brahmins were involved in intellectual pursuits. Today, anyone in academics or policy making would fall under this category. These professions require deep study, deep thinking, authority on the subject, and an ability to guide others. Professional consultants too would fall into this category.

Kshatriyas may be defined as people who protect society from any kind of threat. In the olden days, kingdoms faced attacks by other kingdoms, invaders, and elements like dacoits—all of which are threats to the peaceful life of a society. Kshatriyas are the category of strong men and women, who have the courage and valor to put themselves in the line of fire for others. In the past, this was the job of kings, their commanders, and their armies. Today, our armed forces, police, and other security forces who work for ensuring our security would count as kshatriyas, no matter what the surnames on their nameplates say. In today's hyperconnected world, cyber security experts too would fall under the category of kshatriyas. Anyone who takes on the responsibility of protecting society, even at the cost of his or her own life is a kshatriya.

Vaishyas form the commercial arm of society. So, agriculture, trade, commerce, and industry are managed by this group. They create wealth, and with this wealth, they support the activities of the other three groups. They support brahmins through their charity, which used to be administered through direct patronage in the olden days, but now comes via educational institutes, societies, or trusts. Vaishyas used to pay kings to maintain armies; today they pay taxes that are spent on defense. They patronized art and artists, and paid salaries to those who worked for them. If you read history, you will find that no kingdom has prospered without its vaishya community being prosperous. Kings, kingdoms, wars, art, culture, and education of brahmins—everything was funded by the vaishyas. They were into agriculture, they set up industries, and they traded in products—both man-made and natural—like precious stones, metals, fabrics, spices, and forest products. Today, all entrepreneurs and industrialists would come under this category. If you are working towards enhancing business—yours or that of your employer, you are a vaishya. If you are paying taxes to the government to run the country, you are a vaishya, irrespective of what family you were born into.

Shudras are talented people who do physical work, using their hands and/or bodies to execute the work. They are skilled in what they do. This varna includes manual workers, be it people on the shop floor, people who are building our world by their physical labor, or artists of all kinds, as they too use their skill, and sometimes their body to perform. All the great *shilpis* who built our grand temples and astounding stepwells sporting lovely sculpted stories fall under this category. There may be a hesitation to use the word 'shudra' in today's day and time. Shudra varna simply indicates a category of highly skilled people, with skill sets that people in the other three varnas never had. Shudras of yesteryears had their own, exclusive scriptures, like the shilpa shastras for architects and sculptors. On a related note, Chitrasutra in Vishnudharmottar Puran is a treatise on painting used by painters, while the Natya Shastra is for dancers and performing artists, and so on.

I have read many interpretations of these four categories of varna across all kinds of media. Some interpretations assume the existence of hierarchy in the varna system and hold forth that, based on our karma, we move from one varna to another.

The Purush Sukta from the Rig Veda, while describing the supreme being, says that brahmins are his mouth, kshatriyas his arms, vaishyas his thighs, and shudras his feet. You must remember that this is one of the verses that come up while describing the whole universe that the supreme being spans, which includes celestial bodies like the sun, moon, and space and time, and even animals like horses. So, to understand this one phrase in context, you need to understand the whole genesis of 'Purusha' as described in this sukta. On a twitter thread, a user who goes by the name Parchin Bharat gave me this interesting explanation, "Brahmins are those with universal and expansive minds, Kshatriyas are those with guardian mindset, Vaishyas are focused on business vertically but their operations are global & we do have ample evidence of this from across ages, Shudras are those who have deep local focus." I think this is an angle that encompasses the whole gamut of activities that a society engages in. You can categorize most professions based on varna, and what this helps you achieve is to retain your focus, build your community and improve your expertise in your chosen profession.

As I read history, it seems to me that most literature available to us today was written for the ruling class, but nevertheless, you still see underlined in it, the role of everyone in running the kingdom. The brahmins step in as advisors as and when needed, to train the future kings and other professionals. Vaishyas create industry and shudras contribute by building and through their artworks. We must realize that no matter what we do, we do play a role in society. Some professions may get more limelight or may seem more valuable than the others, but this is just in transient light. For example, my father is a civil engineer who passed out in the 1960s when civil engineers were a much-in-demand breed, as a lot of construction was going on then, in newly independent India. By the time I joined the software industry in the mid-1990s, this industry had emerged as the most coveted profession of that decade. My father told me that he wished he was a software engineer rather than a civil engineer, a profession that had by then lost the prestige it used to have. Today, after a couple of decades, there are so many software professionals around that no one really thinks much of them. Likewise, fifty years back, film stars, especially female film stars were not really respected as much as they are today; today, it is among the most aspired-for professions among youngsters. So then, the relative value of professions does keep changing with time and circumstances. Always remember this *doha* by Rahim—*Rahiman dekh badin ko, laghu na dijiye daari, jahan kaam aave sui, kya kare tarvari*. Never consider your work to be small compared to that of others, for where you need a needle, a sword is useless. So, let us be aware of our place and space in the network of society, and work towards being the best in our chosen fields.

What is purushartha?

Purushartha is a set of four categories that talk about the goals of life. These are not mutually exclusive categories really, as are the categories of varna and ashram. With respect to purushartha, you can pursue all its four goals parallelly, or focus on one or two or three of them at a time. The four purushartha goals or purposes of a human life include:

1. *Dharma*—our duties towards our family, our communities, our society, and most importantly towards ourselves.
2. *Artha*—pursuit of material wealth that helps us and our families lead a comfortable life.
3. *Kama*—the *rasa* or essence of enjoying life, enjoying what your senses enjoy, the pleasures of human life.
4. *Moksha*—the ultimate goal of human life that one should pursue and never forget while pursuing the other three.

I use this framework to judge each of my acts and discern which of the four purushartha goals has been my motive to execute those acts. If I go out to entertain myself—it is to attain kama, and recognizing it as one of the four purushartha goals makes me feel comfortable and allows me to enjoy myself completely without any guilt trip, as I know that this too is one of the purposes in life. If I am pursuing a business deal, I know that I am pursuing my artha goal, to lead a comfortable and independent life. If I am about to cast my vote in the elections to elect my representative in the democratic government, I know this to be my dharma towards society. When I sit down to meditate and focus on my spiritual growth, I know this is my small step towards moksha.

The beauty of purushartha is that it tells you to focus on each of these aspects for a good life, good society, and a good afterlife. It also tells you that material growth is as important as spiritual growth; one need not be a hindrance for the other. It inspires us to strike a balance between the four goals. In fact, some interpretations say that if you follow dharma to earn your artha, you will earn in abundance, which in turn allows you to enjoy kama. Abundance through artha can also become a means to perform larger duties in life, and of course, it helps you enjoy life to the hilt. This reminds me of our deities who get elaborate shringars every day, several times a day, even as they show us the way to spiritual growth. Isn't this a beautiful coming together of dharma, artha, kama and moksha?

Overall, the framework of varna, ashram and purushartha helps us chart our course in life based on our role in family and in society, and based on our personal goals. They help us maintain the much-needed balance in life and add more meaning to our lives.

Which temples should I visit?

I have often been asked this question, mostly when people are visiting temple towns. At times, they have asked me which are the 'x' temples that one should visit in one's lifetime. I am thankful to those who asked this question, for it made me think about it. You obviously cannot visit all possible temples in India or the world. So, how do you choose or decide on which ones to visit, or let us say, which ones to prioritize. So, here is my advice to help you choose the temples.

As a traveler or tourist, you can visit the big and beautiful temples that give you a glimpse of the past grandeur of those destinations. They are a piece of history with their walls telling you many stories. They are the architectural wonders of our past. Few such temples that should be on your travel wish list are the Brihadeeswara Temple in Thanjavur, the Kandariya Mahadev Temple in Khajuraho, the sun temples at Konark in Odisha and Modhera in Gujarat, the Kailashanath Temple at Ellora, the terracotta temples at Bishnupur in Bengal, and the Jain Temple at Ranakpur in Rajasthan. These are some of the most beautiful temples that I have seen. Most of them are under the management of the Archaeological Survey of India, with many of them continuing to be practicing temples. This is just an indicative list, and every traveler will have his or her own list. On the IndiTales Instagram handle you can see a long list of temples that I have seen along with their brief stories to help you choose from a larger spectrum of temples. The wonderful part is, whichever part of India you visit, you will find some ancient temple there to explore. I would recommend that you allot half a day to explore each of them. Even if you are not a devotee, explore them as facets of our common history, or as some of the oldest archaeological heritage out there, which they are.

You could also choose temples based on the architectural styles you wish to explore in detail—like the Chola temples of Tamil Nadu, the Hoysala and Vijayanagara architecture of Karnataka, the wooden temples of Kerala, the terracotta temples of Bengal, the Nagar style temples of Odisha, or the Kathkuni temples of hill states like Uttarakhand and Himachal. Jain temples have their own grace and beauty, especially when you see them exquisitely carved in white marble in the deserts of Rajasthan. Personally, I enjoy the diversity of all these temples. The time in history that interests you could be another parameter employed to choose the temples to visit; for instance, I love to explore 10–11th century temples the most. Each era has its own timestamp.

First, learn the language of Indian art to understand and appreciate our temples. I remember, when I was at the Bhopal Museum which has an amazing collection of sculptures, in its stone sculpture gallery where the sculptures were kept behind a glass barrier, few students were practicing still life photography. I advised them to get the doors opened and some lights switched on to get the right images. This opened a conversation and I asked them if they knew what they were photographing. They drew an absolute blank, for they could not even identify the Shiva and Vishnu murtis in the gallery. Ganesh was the only murti they could identify. So, I gave them a two-minute talk on how to identify the Shiva and Vishnu murtis and some absolute basics of Indian iconography, and I saw a sense of absolute awe on their faces. It was as if something suddenly dawned on them. I could totally identify with the feeling. I had been just like them, a few years back. I do not remember how and when during my travels I started learning and appreciating Indian art, which totally changed the way I looked at India. Every sculpture became a story from the past, a document of history with many facts written on it for the one who could read it. Now, I laugh at those who propagate the myth that Indians did not write down their own history. Indians wrote their history visually, out in the open for anyone to read in any age, regardless of the language that would be in vogue at the time of reading it. If you can spend some time learning the language of Indian iconography, you would have a million stories to read every time you visit an ancient site in India. Thankfully, now, you can learn a lot about Indian art on the Internet. Our blog, IndiTales, has detailed documentation of some of our temples. In our Indian Art series, we explain some of the well-known and common sculptures and artworks of India, like the Nataraja and the wall murals of Ajanta.

Second, do visit your family temples. Most probably, you do have a tradition of visiting your family deity on specific occasions or times of the year. Every family in India has its kul devata and/or kul devi. I would not be surprised if you do not know who they are, but it is not very difficult to find out. Talk to older relatives, ask them which temples are visited after weddings in the family or where rituals like *mundan* are performed, and this would probably be at your family temple. Family deities have been worshipped since eons by our ancestors and visiting them and worshipping them is akin to upholding our family traditions. And then, if you dig deep, you may discover family history associated with the temple or the deity, or with both. Sometimes, the family deity happens to be an illustrious ancestor as in the case of the Charan community of Rajasthan who worship their ancestor Karni Mata.

The Karni Mata temple at Deshnoke near Bikaner is more popularly known as the Rat Temple. The temple, though it is open to anyone who wants to visit it, belongs to the Charan community. Karni Mata is an ancestor of this community who lived in the late 14th or early 15th century. She performed courageous deeds which safeguarded the community from certain major disasters. As time passed, these incredible acts of courage started being seen as miracles, and Karni Mata became a deity. As a matter of fact, worshipping of ancestors is a common practice in all ancient communities. Even today, we observe *pitr paksha,* the fortnight dedicated to remembering and praying to our ancestors. Going back to the Charans, all of them trace their ancestry to Karni Mata or her family. She is their kul devi, and the supreme Devi for them. Even the royal family of Bikaner has her as the kul devi. Similarly, it could be quite interesting and rewarding to dig up the history of your own family deity and discover how your lineage is associated with the deity.

Third, visit the kshetra devatas of the region you travel to. Every region in India—including every city, town, and village—has a presiding deity. They are like the heads of families, if you regard the city, town, or village as a family. Visiting them is like paying respect to elders of the family. More often than not, these deities are closely associated with the history of their respective locations. Quiz the city's folks and you will get to hear legends and tales associated with these deities. For example, the city of Kolhapur regales you with tales of the killing of the asura, Kolhasur, by Mahalakshmi; the town of Sringeri in Karnataka reminds you of Shringi Rishi who lived there once, and for being the place that Adi Shankaracharya chose for his first matha.

On a different note, when I wrote a post on the various terms of greetings that we use across India, I discovered that apart from the generic namaste and namaskar, most regions use specific greeting phrases that celebrate the presiding or *adhishtra devatas* of those regions. In Puri, they say 'Jai Jagannath'; in Braj, it is always 'Radhe Radhe'; in Gujarat, it is 'Jai Sri Krishna', while Jains say 'Jai Jinendra'. Evidently, the inherent culture of a place revolves around its presiding deity.

So, if you are visiting Varanasi, you must visit the Vishwanath Temple and the Annapurna Temple. If you are a serious traveler to Kashi, include a visit to the Kedareshwar and the Omkareshwar temples along with the Bindu Madhav Temple and the Shaktipeeth Vishalakshi Devi Temple. If you are in Ujjain, your visit to the city is not complete without visiting the Mahakaal Temple that has been at the heart of the city ever since the city began to exist. If you are in Kanchipuram, there is no way you can miss visiting the presiding devi of the city—Kamakshi Amman; even the Shiva and Vishnu temples surround her temple in this city.

There are also the temples of the *gram* devis and gram devatas to consider. In south Indian villages, you will see these temples right at the center of the village, with roads emanating from the temple. In North India, such sacred geography of towns and cities is more or less lost, but you will still find some traces of it. At many places, the kshetra devatas, kul devatas and gram devatas could be one and the same.

Finally, visit your ishta devata. Ishta devata is the deity you connect with most, the one you worship, your own chosen personal deity. This may or may not be same as your kshetra devata or your kul devata. For example, you could live in Kashi and still connect with Hanuman or Ganapati the most. Whoever your ishta devata is, try and visit the places associated with that deity. In fact, as a devotee of your ishta devata, you would be naturally inclined to visit these places. So, if you believe in Venkateshwara, then visiting his shrine on the Tirumala Hills is bound to be on your wish list. You could also visit the places associated with your ishta devata across the country. For instance, if you pray to Shiva, you could visit the twelve Jyotirlingas that would take you from the Himalayas in the North to the Ram Setu in the south, from Somnath in the west to Vaidyanath in the east. There is a longer list of 108 Shiva kshetras to explore, though they tend to be concentrated in South India. If you are a Vaishnavite, you could visit the 108 *divyadesams* associated with Vishnu. If you connect with Ram, you could visit Ayodhya, Mithila, Panchvati and Sri Lanka. If Krishna steals your heart, go see his playground in Mathura and Vrindavan, or visit the golden city he built at Dwarka on the western margins of India, or Puri where he lives with his siblings. If you are a Devi bhakta, the choice is ample—there are fifty-one or 108 Shaktipeethas across the Indian subcontinent. If you love Ganesha, visit the Ashtvinayaks of Maharashtra. The choices are endless.

Finally, listen to your heart and visit the places that you are naturally attracted to. It could be a temple in your neighborhood or the puja alcove in your own house. Some of us worship the *nirguna rupa,* wherein the deity has no physical form, we meditate upon the all-pervading Brahman from which everything emanates.

Which devata should I pray to?

33 million deities—the number seems mind boggling. Is it even possible to know all of them? Obviously not.

Is it possible to understand them? Definitely, yes, if you understand who it is that we call a devata.

We call our parents, including the ones who give birth to us and the ones who raise us, as our devatas. Our teachers who teach us and prepare us for life are our devatas. Similarly, anyone who helps us in life, especially our mentors in life can be our devatas. Having said that, your devata need not be my devata. Your parents are your devatas, my parents are mine, and the same logic applies to the rest of your personal devatas.

Adi Shankaracharya made it easy for us to make our choices when he introduced '*Shanmat*' or the six main paths that a Hindu can choose from. Each of these paths has a presiding deity—Shiva, Vishnu, Shakti, Ganesh, Karthik and Surya. You can choose any one of them as your ishta devata. He considered these six deities as the manifestations of the same Brahman—the all-pervading consciousness which is nirguna or without any form. Since most of us cannot comprehend a formless supreme consciousness, we can choose from among any one of these forms and still reach the same Brahman.

If you are perplexed about which deity is better than the other, the answer is, all of them are just manifestations of the one that cannot be defined by *rupa-bheda*. Nirguna is one that cannot be depicted by drawing or sculpting a form. If you are still confused about who among these deities—Shiva, Vishnu, Brahma, Shakti, Ganesh, Karthik and Surya —is the most powerful, the answer is, for you, the most powerful one is the one you choose to worship.

In Indian thought, deities as well as societies operate on a network model, rather than a hierarchical model. If you read the stories of any of these deities, you will find that they are always shown dependent on each other. You will rarely find a story that features just one of them. The path you choose to follow decides just your protagonist; the one through whose eyes you would listen to the stories. If you choose Shiva, he becomes your protagonist and the stories highlighted are the ones in which he emerges as the supreme deity. The same goes for the other manifestations we admire. At a societal level too, who is important is dependent on what is collectively called '*desh kaal paristhiti*' meaning 'space, time and circumstances'. Who is most important depends on where you are, the timeframe under consideration, and what is going on then. For example, at an event, the speaker is the most important person as he or she is sharing the knowledge that the others are attempting to receive. However, if the hall's electricity supply hits a hitch, the electrician, who may otherwise have had no role to play, becomes the most important person for the event to be continued. Similarly, if a medical emergency crops up in the auditorium, the doctor at the hospital becomes the most sought-after person, but even before that, it is the ambulance and its driver who are more important. So, the world, while it might seem to be operating with some pre-conceived hierarchies, is actually a network of inter-dependent entities. Once we realize this, our lives become easier, as we no longer run after perceived social hierarchies which are more of ego boosters.

Let me end this chapter by sharing my favorite tenet from the Indian thought system. It is the triad of *icchashakti-gyanshakti-kriyashakti*. To achieve anything, you need three kinds of powers—it all begins with the strong will to do or create something, the power of knowledge to achieve it, and finally the power of action to do it. Recognize that all the three powers are there within you, with that, there would be nothing that can stop you. If you keep this in mind, you will achieve all that you set out to achieve, at the right time and place.

Until Our Paths Cross Again

पद्मप्रिये पद्मिनि पद्महस्ते पद्मालये पद्मदलायताक्षि ।
विश्वप्रिये विष्णु मनोऽनुकूले त्वत्पादपद्मं मयि सन्निधत्स्व ॥२४॥

—Sri Suktam

The one whom the lotus loves, one who is herself the lotus, who holds a lotus in her hands, who lives in the abode of the lotus, whose eyes are like lotus petals, who creates the world as Vishnu wishes, give me a place close to your feet.

This has been my journey so far, of discovering the sacred and eternal in India. Along the way, I discovered the invisible threads that connect and sew India together, threads which revealed themselves to me enchantingly, like the opening of a thousand-petaled lotus, one petal at a time. I found the same threads forging connections within me, somewhere deep down. These travels kept introducing me to the knowledge I inherited inherently by taking birth in this land, and by living in many different parts of this country. Each step I took on the outside opened many windows on the inside for me. All these rendezvous keep reminding me that I am part of a continuum whose baton is in my hands at this moment, a baton I must pass on after adding my own experiences to the continuum.

I would never be able to thank all the people who have knowingly or unknowingly shared their knowledge and wisdom with me—both online and on the road. Most of them are unaware of the contribution they have made to my life. The people, and the places, I encountered during my travels—I can never put an adequate value to what I have gained from both, it has been an invaluable experience. Even the scattered memories and ruminations on those encounters leave me richer.

It is one thing to read phrases and idioms in textbooks, however when you see them live in front of your eyes is when you really internalize them. At Chandratal—the holy lake located fifteen thousand feet above mean sea level, I saw a herd of sheep following their leader blindly as they crossed small rivulets and wandered on the grassy patches of the barren hills with snowy peaks. This is when I understood the meaning of *bhed-chaal* or herd mentality, of people blindly following the leader. However, it also gave me a glimpse into leadership—if you take the first steps confidently, people will put their faith in you and follow you. In fact, they will not just follow you but will also support you in myriad ways. This has been a learning that has stood me in good stead. Many such things that were mere theory to me for a long time, came alive during my travels and left me richer, with insights.

I remember, once, I was trying to locate a place associated with Indra around the Govardhan Parvat near Mathura. The legend of Govardhan is after all connected with the tiff between Krishna and Indra. After asking about twenty-thirty people in vain, I was about to lose hope when a young girl walked up to me and said: Let me show you. She spent the next few hours taking me along on an in-depth tour of the Govardhan Parikrama, explaining that every temple, every pond, and every stone there is nothing but Govardhan ji. Her immense faith in Krishna and her lived experience of doing the Dandwat Parikrama every year made my visit so much more meaningful. When she told me stories from scriptures and from folklore, she was like a Gopika who has seen it all with her own eyes. What a contrast she drew with the approved guide accompanying me, who knew and articulated nothing beyond the two famous temples of the place, despite being a local resident himself.

At Kolhapur, a twitter follower guided me online to visit the little-known gems of the cultural nerve center of Maharashtra. At Chandratal, our host regaled us with ghost stories under the starry sky in the biting cold. At Dwarka, my driver, seeing me struggle to find answers to my questions, took me home to meet his 92-year-old grandfather, a librarian. At Kanchipuram, the Shankaracharya ji at Kanchi Matha took me under his wings and ensured I got to know the city of Kanchipuram as intimately as possible. At the Kumbh Mela, Swami Vishokananda ji guided me with his insights on yatras. A number of pujaris and archaks from temples shared their knowledge and blessed me. Each of these magical interventions are blessings that continue to guide me on my travels.

People have welcomed me into their homes, into temples' inner sanctums that are not open to the public, into their hearts, and have given me so much. I feel special, but I know that I am in no way special. You could say that it is my strong ichhashakti, my willpower, that kept me going, or you could simply call me fortunate and blessed. The only things I have been doing consistently are—stepping out, stepping into ambiguity, and letting the universe guide me. And the universe did guide me, better than I could have ever planned it myself. Martin Luther King Jr. famously said, "To other countries I may go as a tourist, but to India I come as a pilgrim." Well, my experiences transformed me into a pilgrim from being just another curious traveler.

Every place that I have stayed in, I have established a bond with it. I have left a bit of me there, and a bit of it became a part of me. Every time I visited an ancient land, it whispered some stories to me, and it opened some windows in my mind. It gave me glimpses of the knowledge and wisdom codified in our language, literature, folklore and of course, in our temples. Every journey helped me grow, helped me expand. No place that I have visited feels alien, they all feel like mine; a part of me lives there. Is that not what a pilgrimage does, it takes you out of your home and makes you a part of the larger universe. Your horizon expands with every new place, every new conversation. There is no bigger university in life than travel. It teaches you first-hand in a way that every learning becomes a part of you.

At some point in time, I started giving more importance to my own first-hand experience than to what I learn from others' experiences or commentaries. I do use data from earlier documentations and chronicles, but I go by my own experience. I converse with the destinations, and they always oblige by sharing their secrets.

Gradually, lot of dots started getting connected, leaving me thrilled and illuminated. It is like having a circuit board in my mind, and suddenly bulbs light up, showing new connections between seemingly unrelated things. Often, this happens in the quietest of moments. I have started seeing the patterns that show how different places are connected and are sometimes even conversing with each other. If this could happen to me, I can only imagine and marvel at the insights that someone like Adi Shankaracharya or Chaitanya Mahaprabhu or Guru Nanak Dev would have received when they walked the length and breadth of this country.

The way I look at India has changed over time, in light of discovering the sacred and eternal within her. All the places I visited feel like extensions of my own soul. India never ceases to amaze me, and this is my biggest motive to keep traveling and to keep exploring her.

Acknowledgements

This book comes from years of traveling across India, reading books on India—from ancient scriptures to modern renditions, and correlating both. So, my first 'Thank you' goes to everyone I met on the road, to every conversation, to every interaction that gave me insight, and to every experience that helped me write this book. Some of you get a mention in the book, but this book also owes to innumerable others who remain nameless.

My second 'Thank you' is to all the authors I read, who opened windows for me to explore. You gave me all the right nudges to step out and explore India.

I also want to thank my blog (IndiTales) readers and social media family for all their affection and support, and more importantly, for sharing their knowledge whole-heartedly with me. In fact, my Hindi readers have been asking me for a book for a few years now. I owe one to them.

Several of my travels were supported by state tourism boards and hospitality brands across the country. A big shout-out to them, may you prosper many times over.

Your spouse is your co-writer in many ways. He or she frees up the time you need to write by supporting you in a million ways. However, in the case of this book, the very idea for it came from my husband. Shashi is the first listener of all my travel experiences, and at some point in time, he began telling me that I must put all of it together in a book;

he was convinced that more people ought to know these aspects of India. So, this book has really come out of his nudging me to organize my thoughts and experiences for a larger audience. My only worry is, he keeps coming up with more such ideas.

My thanks to my friends Milind and Madhumita Tamhane, who were the first readers of this book, and I must say, they were very encouraging readers. Thank you Hema Singh for being my most dependable sounding board ever, your feedback inspired the title and the cover. Thank you, Ramakrishna Kongalla ji, for helping me out with the Sanskrit quote from the shilpa shastras.

Thank you Sankrant Sanu for sending me that email, which any author would love to receive from a publisher, especially when there is no history of a working relationship yet. It is frame worthy. Thank you Hema Vijay for editing the book affectionately like your own. Thank you, team Garuda, may the people riding with you be the source of Sri and Srinath for you.

Glossary

Dargah	A place associated with holy men who follow Islam or Sufism.
Japa	A pre-defined number of chants of a particular mantra—typically 108.
Kali	Kali means black but can also be used to tease.
Janmashtami	Janmashtami is Sri Krishna's birthday that falls on the eighth day of the waning moon fortnight of the lunar month of Bhadrapad, roughly falling in early September.
Navaratri	Navaratri refers to the nine nights that are dedicated to the Devi; it occurs twice a year, but the most important one occurs during the month of Ashwin and roughly falls in early October.
Ishta devata	Personal deity whom one follows.
Kshetra	Region that a deity presides over.
Dahi bhat	Rice and curd dish.
Pran pratishtha	Sculptor opens the eyes of the deity, and after this, the murti is considered a living being. The term used is pran pratishtha.
Kos	1 Kos = 3.12 kilometers.
Panda	A pandit.

Iccha Swayamvara	A type of swayamvara wherein the girl chooses the groom she wants from among those participating in the swayamvara.
Sthapati	Traditional Indian architect.
Chaupar	An ancient board game that was also played in the Mahabharata.
Mundu	A sarong–an unstitched piece of cloth.
Tirtham	Water poured on the deities during daily rituals and given to devotees as prasad.
Nati	Acrobat.

Select Bibliography

- Osho. *India My Love.*
- Jain, Meenakshi. *Flight of Deities and Rebirth of Temples.*
- Mishra, Anupam. *Aaj Bhi Khare Hain Talab.*
- Misra, Nityananda. *Kumbha – Traditionally Modern Mela.*
- *Tirthank.* Gita Press.
- *Devi Bhagwat Mahapuran.* Gita Press.
- *Sankshipt Skand Puran.* Gita Press.
- Dr. Dehejia, Vidya. *Modes of Narration in Buddhist Art.*
- Kapur, Anuradha. *Actors, Pilgrims, Kings and Gods – The Ramlila of Ramnagar.*
- Lahiri, Nayanjot. *Time Pieces – A Whistle Stop Tour of Ancient India.*
- Sharan, Mishi. *Chasing the Monk's Shadow.*
- Iyengar, R. N., Kannan, K. S., & Wakankar, S. Y. *Narada Silpasastra - Sanskrit Text on Architectural Civil Engineering.*
- Singh, Rana P.B. (1991), Rāma's route after banishment: a geographical viewpoint. *Journal of Scientific Research* (Banaras Hindu University, Varanasi, ISSN: 0447-9483), <BHU Platinum Jubilee Year>, Special Volume, 41 (B): pp. 39-46. [author's Web. Ref. Pdf, 085.91].
- https://twitter.com/Swamy39/status/1219762153852243968?s=20
- https://www.business-standard.com/article/pti-stories/kullu-s-raghunath-temple-to-remain-royal-family-property-sc-118012901392_1.html

- https://www.scribd.com/document/100741462/International-Seminar-on-the-Cultural-Linkage-Between-Ayodhya-India-Aytthya-Thailand
- https://www.researchgate.net/publication/2180120_Concepts_of_Space_Time_and_Consciousness_in_Ancient_India
- https://en.wikipedia.org/wiki/Koothu
- https://en.wikipedia.org/wiki/Junagadh_rock_inscription_of_Rudradaman
- http://www.assaminfo.com/tourist-places/25/namdang-stone-bridge.htm
- https://ia802600.us.archive.org/11/items/AntiquarianInterestsInMedievalIndiaTheRelocationOfPillarsByFiruzshahAntiquarianInterestsInMedievalIndia.pdf
- https://kavitakosh.org/

GARUDA PRAKASHAN BOOKS

GARUDA PRAKASHAN BOOKS